Tobacco and Smoking

Opposing Viewpoints®

OTHER BOOKS OF RELATED INTEREST

OPPOSING VIEWPOINTS SERIES

Alcohol
Chemical Dependency
Drug Abuse
Health and Fitness
The War on Drugs

CURRENT CONTROVERSIES SERIES

Alcoholism
Drug Trafficking
Gambling
Illegal Drugs
Smoking
Teen Addiction

AT ISSUE SERIES

Legalizing Drugs
Smoking

Tobacco and Smoking

Opposing Viewpoints®

David L. Bender, *Publisher*
Bruno Leone, *Executive Editor*
Bonnie Szumski, *Editorial Director*
Brenda Stalcup, *Managing Editor*
Scott Barbour, *Senior Editor*
Mary E. Williams, *Book Editor*
Tamara L. Roleff, *Book Editor*
Charles P. Cozic, *Assistant Editor*

OPPOSING
VIEWPOINTS®
SERIES

Greenhaven Press, Inc., San Diego, California

Cover photo: Dave Allen

Library of Congress Cataloging-in-Publication Data

Tobacco and smoking : opposing viewpoints / Mary E. Williams, book
    editor, Tamara L. Roleff, book editor, Charles P. Cozic, assistant
    editor.
        p.   cm. — (Opposing viewpoints series)
    Includes bibliographical references and index.
    ISBN 1-56510-803-5 (: alk. paper). —
ISBN 1-56510-802-7 (pbk. : alk. paper)
    1. Tobacco habit—United States. 2. Cigarette habit—United States.
3. Smoking—United States. 4. Tobacco industry—United States.
I. Williams, Mary E., 1960–   . II. Roleff, Tamara L., 1959–   .
III. Cozic, Charles P., 1957–   . IV. Series: Opposing viewpoints series
(Unnumbered)
HV5760.T63 1998
362.29'6—dc21   97-51730
                                                                          CIP

Greenhaven Press, Inc., P.O. Box 289009
San Diego, CA 92198-9009

"CONGRESS SHALL MAKE NO LAW...ABRIDGING THE FREEDOM OF SPEECH, OR OF THE PRESS."

First Amendment to the U.S. Constitution

The basic foundation of our democracy is the First Amendment guarantee of freedom of expression. The Opposing Viewpoints Series is dedicated to the concept of this basic freedom and the idea that it is more important to practice it than to enshrine it.

CONTENTS

Chapter 3: Should the Government Regulate Smoking and Tobacco?

Chapter 4: Should Tobacco Companies Be Sanctioned?

WHY CONSIDER
OPPOSING VIEWPOINTS?

"The only way in which a human being can make some
approach to knowing the whole of a subject is by hearing
what can be said about it by persons of every variety of
opinion and studying all modes in which it can be looked
at by every character of mind. No wise man ever acquired
his wisdom in any mode but this."

John Stuart Mill

In our media-intensive culture it is not difficult to find differing
opinions. Thousands of newspapers and magazines and dozens
of radio and television talk shows resound with differing points
of view. The difficulty lies in deciding which opinion to agree
with and which "experts" seem the most credible. The more in-
undated we become with differing opinions and claims, the
more essential it is to hone critical reading and thinking skills to
evaluate these ideas. Opposing Viewpoints books address this
problem directly by presenting stimulating debates that can be
used to enhance and teach these skills. The varied opinions contained in each book examine many different aspects of a single
issue. While examining these conveniently edited opposing
views, readers can develop critical thinking skills such as the
ability to compare and contrast authors' credibility, facts, argu-
mentation styles, use of persuasive techniques, and other stylis-
tic tools. In short, the Opposing Viewpoints Series is an ideal
way to attain the higher-level thinking and reading skills so essential in a culture of diverse and contradictory opinions.

In addition to providing a tool for critical thinking, Opposing
Viewpoints books challenge readers to question their own
strongly held opinions and assumptions. Most people form their
opinions on the basis of upbringing, peer pressure, and personal, cultural, or professional bias. By reading carefully balanced opposing views, readers must directly confront new ideas
as well as the opinions of those with whom they disagree. This
is not to simplistically argue that everyone who reads opposing
views will—or should—change his or her opinion. Instead, the
series enhances readers' understanding of their own views by
encouraging confrontation with opposing ideas. Careful examination of others' views can lead to the readers' understanding of
the logical inconsistencies in their own opinions, perspective on

why they hold an opinion, and the consideration of the possibility that their opinion requires further evaluation.

EVALUATING OTHER OPINIONS

To ensure that this type of examination occurs, Opposing Viewpoints books present all types of opinions. Prominent spokespeople on different sides of each issue as well as well-known professionals from many disciplines challenge the reader. An additional goal of the series is to provide a forum for other, less known, or even unpopular viewpoints. The opinion of an ordinary person who has had to make the decision to cut off life support from a terminally ill relative, for example, may be just as valuable and provide just as much insight as a medical ethicist's professional opinion. The editors have two additional purposes in including these less known views. One, the editors encourage readers to respect others' opinions—even when not enhanced by professional credibility. It is only by reading or listening to and objectively evaluating others' ideas that one can determine whether they are worthy of consideration. Two, the inclusion of such viewpoints encourages the important critical thinking skill of objectively evaluating an author's credentials and bias. This evaluation will illuminate an author's reasons for taking a particular stance on an issue and will aid in readers' evaluation of the author's ideas.

As series editors of the Opposing Viewpoints Series, it is our hope that these books will give readers a deeper understanding of the issues debated and an appreciation of the complexity of even seemingly simple issues when good and honest people disagree. This awareness is particularly important in a democratic society such as ours in which people enter into public debate to determine the common good. Those with whom one disagrees should not be regarded as enemies but rather as people whose views deserve careful examination and may shed light on one's own.

Thomas Jefferson once said that "difference of opinion leads to inquiry, and inquiry to truth." Jefferson, a broadly educated man, argued that "if a nation expects to be ignorant and free . . . it expects what never was and never will be." As individuals and as a nation, it is imperative that we consider the opinions of others and examine them with skill and discernment. The Opposing Viewpoints Series is intended to help readers achieve this goal.

David L. Bender & Bruno Leone,
Series Editors

Greenhaven Press anthologies primarily consist of previously published material taken from a variety of sources, including periodicals, books, scholarly journals, newspapers, government documents, and position papers from private and public organizations. These original sources are often edited for length and to ensure their accessibility for a young adult audience. The anthology editors also change the original titles of these works in order to clearly present the main thesis of each viewpoint and to explicitly indicate the opinion presented in the viewpoint. These alterations are made in consideration of both the reading and comprehension levels of a young adult audience. Every effort is made to ensure that Greenhaven Press accurately reflects the original intent of the authors included in this anthology.

INTRODUCTION

"For decades, [tobacco] industry strategy was to deny everything and create uncertainty about tobacco's deadly effects and the addictiveness of nicotine."

—Henry A.Waxman

"Millions of people, knowing the risks, choose to smoke anyway."

—Mona Charen

When a smoker takes a puff from a cigarette, the bloodstream quickly absorbs nicotine through the lungs and distributes it throughout the body. In about ten seconds, nicotine reaches nerve-cell "nicotine receptors" in the brain, causing the secretion of dopamine, a chemical that creates feelings of pleasure. Other brain chemicals, including norepinephrine (inducing energy and alertness) and endorphins (causing relaxation and pain relief) are also released, creating the mental clarity and calmness that smokers enjoy. The habit of cigarette smoking, however, is dangerous. Smoking causes cancer, cardiovascular disease, and emphysema; it also can contribute to birth defects and respiratory illnesses in children. According to the U.S. Centers for Disease Control and Prevention, 400,000 people die each year from smoking-related diseases—more than the annual deaths caused by alcohol, AIDS, traffic accidents, drug abuse, murder, and suicide combined.

In light of this information, many scientists, health organizations, and consumer advocates charge that the tobacco industry should be held responsible for the illnesses and deaths caused by smoking. Tobacco critics maintain, for one thing, that cigarette manufacturers and their lawyers suppressed evidence and deceived the public for decades about the dangers of smoking. Despite the surgeon general's warning label about the hazards of tobacco use—required on all packs of cigarettes after 1965—the attractive images and lifestyles depicted in tobacco ads effectively persuaded people to smoke, tobacco opponents contend. In the 1990s, such criticism against the tobacco industry culminated in several lawsuits agains cigarette manufacturers to recoup the costs of treating smoking-related illnesses. Moreover, many plaintiffs in these suits accuse tobacco manufacturers of secretly manipulating nicotine levels in cigarettes to "hook" more smokers and keep them addicted—thereby ensuring future profits for the tobacco industry. For example, Richard Hurt, the director of the Mayo Clinic's Nicotine Dependence Center, testified in a 1998 Minnesota lawsuit that the tobacco industry intentionally capitalized on the addictive properties of nicotine. Hurt, who had read just-released tobacco industry documents before his testimony, asserted that cigarette manufacturers have considered nicotine to be a drug for many decades. These manufacturers also experimented with ammonia additives to create an enhanced and more easily absorbed form of nicotine, Hurt argued. Because nicotine gives users "cravings that eventually become nearly impossible to deny," Hurt and many other dependency experts have had to treat smokers with techniques similar to those used to treat other substance addictions. He contends, however, that such methods are effective for only 20 percent of smokers. "The tendency is to blame the smoker [for cigarette addiction]," Hurt said. "The smoker isn't the problem. The drug is the problem. . . . Smokers are ordinary people who are controlled by a drug."

Not everyone agrees that the tobacco industry should be held solely responsible for the addictions and illnesses associated with cigarette smoking, however. Robert Levy, senior fellow in constitutional studies at the Cato Institute, points out that the public has long been aware of the dangers of smoking: "The hazards of tobacco were well-documented as long as 400 years ago. Indeed, throughout [the twentieth] century incessant warnings have emanated from thousands of health publications, medical professionals, and government entities." People choose to smoke even though they are fully informed about tobacco's dangers, Levy argues; therefore, they must take responsibility for the consequences of their choice. Others contend, furthermore, that smokers are not the victims of a conspiracy by the tobacco industry to turn people into nicotine addicts. As business professor Richard McKenzie points out, "Addicted smokers were not always so: At some point, they had a choice about whether to go down the addictive path of smoking." The claim that nicotine addiction is an almost insurmountable obstacle is actually an attempt by antitobacco groups to downplay the significance of individual responsibility, several commentators contend. According to syndicated columnist Leonard Larsen, for instance, "addiction peddlers" remove the burden of personal choice, "bolstering those 'can't quit' smokers with a fiction that they're 'hooked' and without hope of quitting on their own." In actuality, 46 million smokers have managed to quit—a fact that proves to many observers that people are responsible for their own decisions to consume—or to stop consuming—health-damaging products.

The addictiveness of tobacco and the relative responsibility of individual smokers are among the issues examined in *Tobacco and Smoking: Opposing Viewpoints*, which includes the following chapters: Are Tobacco Products Harmful? Should Tobacco Advertising Be Restricted? Should the Government Regulate Smoking and Tobacco? Should Tobacco Companies Be Sanctioned? Throughout these chapters, authors debate the health effects of tobacco use as well as the responses of scientists, industry supporters, consumer advocates, lawmakers, and government officials to the continued manufacturing and consumption of tobacco products.

CHAPTER 1

ARE TOBACCO PRODUCTS HARMFUL?

CHAPTER PREFACE

In January 1993, the Environmental Protection Agency (EPA) issued a report declaring that environmental tobacco smoke—secondhand smoke—is a carcinogen that damages the health of nonsmokers. According to the EPA, secondhand smoke is responsible for 37,000 heart disease deaths, 3,000 lung cancer deaths, and 10,000 deaths from other cancers in U.S. nonsmokers each year. This conclusion was drawn from the results of thirty epidemiologic studies, including eleven surveys conducted in the United States. Various other lung cancer investigations support the EPA's claims. Two independent 1992 studies, for example, concluded that nonsmoking women whose husbands smoke face a significantly increased risk of lung cancer. A 1994 survey of nonsmoking women conducted by Elizabeth Fontham found a 24 percent increase in lung cancer risk due to household exposure to cigarette smoke, a 39 percent increased risk due to workplace exposure, and a 50 percent increased risk for exposure in social settings. While none of these studies claim that minimal exposure to environmental tobacco smoke presents a serious health hazard, experts point out that those who live or work with smokers are at greater risk for developing cancer than those who are rarely exposed.

Several critics, however, disagree with the EPA and other investigators who link environmental tobacco smoke to cancer. For example, one major U.S. study published in the November 1992 *American Journal of Public Health* did not find any substantial connection between secondhand smoke and lung cancer. Other analysts criticize the EPA studies for failing to consider several variables other than environmental tobacco smoke that could cause cancer. The Congressional Research Service, for instance, points out that "if wives of smokers share [with smokers] in poor health habits or other factors that could contribute to illness, statistical associations found between disease and passive smoking could be incidental or misleading." These critics conclude, therefore, that the cancer risks associated with secondhand smoke have been exaggerated.

Whether cigarette smoke and nicotine endangers human health remains controversial. The authors in the following chapter present several arguments on the health effects of tobacco use.

| "Smoking remains the leading cause of preventable death in the United States."

CIGARETTE SMOKING IS HARMFUL

American Thoracic Society

Cigarette smoking damages human health, argues the American Thoracic Society (ATS) in the following viewpoint. According to the ATS, smoking is a major cause of lung cancer and cardiovascular disease and can be a contributing factor to birth defects, childhood respiratory illnesses, and several forms of cancer. Policymakers must develop effective antismoking campaigns to reduce the number of preventable deaths caused by cigarette smoking, asserts the ATS. The American Thoracic Society is the medical division of the American Lung Association.

As you read, consider the following questions:

1. According to the ATS, how many Americans died of smoking-related diseases in 1990?
2. What health risks are associated with smoking during pregnancy, according to the ATS?
3. What are the symptoms of nicotine withdrawal syndrome, according to the authors?

Knowledge about the adverse health effects of cigarette smoking has accumulated for more than four decades. Since the first report of the U.S. Surgeon General in 1964 causally linking cigarette smoking with the development of lung cancer, numerous scientific studies and summary reports have been published that document the contribution of cigarette smoking to morbidity and mortality from a variety of conditions. Although the prevalence of cigarette use has and continues to decline, smoking remains the leading cause of preventable death in the United States.

In 1985, the American Thoracic Society (ATS) first issued a position statement titled "Cigarette Smoking and Health," which reviewed the adverse health consequences of smoking known at that time. During the years since this initial statement, considerable scientific evidence has emerged confirming the findings of the initial report, expanding the number of conditions known to be caused or worsened by smoking, and describing the biological mechanisms by which smoking causes adverse health effects. Furthermore, passive inhalation of environmental tobacco smoke (ETS) by nonsmokers has been associated with many of the same health consequences as active smoking, albeit with much smaller degrees of increased risk, and has recently been classified by the Environmental Protection Agency as a Class A (known human) carcinogen.

As in the 1985 ATS statement on smoking, the conclusions reached here are based on the total weight of scientific data and consensus opinion. This evidence derives both from laboratory studies and from epidemiologic studies of human populations, with causal inferences bases on the consistency, reproducibility, and strength of associations, as well as the presence of an exposure-response relationship.

THE PREVALENCE OF CIGARETTE SMOKING

The prevalence of cigarette smoking in the United States has decreased since 1964, when the first Surgeon General's *Report on Smoking and Health* was published. In 1965, 52% of men and 34% of women over age 18 were cigarette smokers. By 1991, these percentages had decreased to 28% for men and 24% for women. Similarly, per capita cigarette consumption (for adults over age 18) peaked in 1963 at 4,345 and by 1992 had decreased 39% to 2,640. Still, cigarette smoking among younger people remains a major public health concern. Nearly all first use of tobacco occurs before high school graduation, and each day 3,000 teenagers start to smoke. Among high school seniors, the prevalence of daily cigarette smoking, which was 29% in 1976, has remained in the 17 to 19% range since 1984. Despite an overall decline in the number of smokers in the United States and much of the developed world, the prevalence of cigarette smoking continues to increase in many developing countries.

Cigarette smoking is very costly to both the individual and society. New long-term studies estimate that about half of all regular cigarette smokers will eventually be killed by their habit. In 1993 the estimated smoking-attributable costs for medical care were $50 billion. When lost work and productivity were added, the total cost to society was estimated to exceed $97 billion, or $373 per capita. If these costs were borne by smokers in the form of cigarette taxes, the price of each pack of cigarettes would have to rise $4.

The Health Risks of Smoking

Cigarette smoking is a major contributor to mortality in the United States. In 1990, approximately 440,000 Americans died from diseases directly related to cigarette smoking. More impressively, at that time more than one out of every five deaths was the result of smoking. The American Cancer Society's Cancer Prevention Study II, a prospective evaluation of almost 1.2 million men and women from 1982–1986, found that the overall mortality ratio (i.e., deaths from all causes in current smokers compared to deaths in those who never smoked) was 2.22 for men smoking 1 to 20 cigarettes a day and 2.43 for men smoking 21 or more cigarettes a day. Similarly, the mortality ratio was 1.60 and 2.10, respectively, for women smoking 1 to 19 and 20 or more cigarettes a day. Cigarette smoking remains the most preventable cause of premature death in the United States. It has been estimated, for example, that a heavy smoker at age 25 can expect a life expectancy at least 25% shorter than a nonsmoker.

Cigarette smokers also have greater morbidity than nonsmokers. Current smokers have more acute and chronic illness as well as more restricted activity days, more bed disability days, and more school and work absenteeism than former smokers or those who never smoked. . . .

Lung Cancer

The 1964 Surgeon General's report concluded that cigarette smoking was causally related to lung cancer. Since then, irrefutable evidence has documented that cigarette smoking is the major cause of lung cancer of each of the principal histologic types (i.e., epidermoid, small cell, large cell, and adenocarcinoma) for both men and women. In 1991, there were 161,000 new cases of lung cancer and 143,000 deaths from lung cancer.

The amount and duration of smoking determine the risk of lung cancer for individual smokers. Men or women who smoke 40 or more cigarettes a day have twice the lung cancer risk of those who smoke 20 or less cigarettes a day. Individuals who start smoking before the age of 15 are four times more likely to develop lung cancer than those who begin after the age of 25. Epidemiologic studies have shown that brands of cigarettes that contain less tar and nicotine only marginally reduce the risk of lung cancer mortality. Similarly, little difference in mortality have been found for lifelong filter versus nonfilter smokers and for persistent smokers who switch from nonfilter to filter cigarettes.

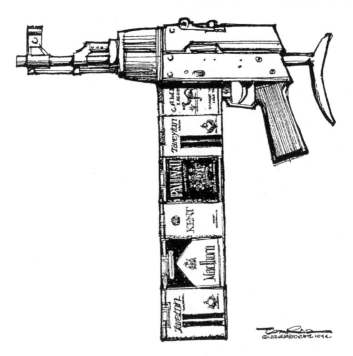

Paul Conrad, © 1997, Los Angeles Times. Reprinted with permission.

During the last several years, lung cancer mortality has stabilized in men but continues to rise dramatically in women. Presently, lung cancer is the leading cause of cancer deaths in women, a distinction that is largely attributable to an earlier age at smoking initiation and a greater number of cigarettes smoked per day than previously reported.

The exact mechanism by which cigarette smoking causes lung cancer is not fully understood. A multistage model in which smoking sequentially transforms cells from normal to malignant is widely accepted. The components of tobacco smoke have been proven capable of initiating and promoting such a process of carcinogenesis.

Several host and environmental factors may influence the risk of lung cancer in cigarette smokers. A family history of lung cancer and exposure to radon or asbestos greatly increase the likelihood of lung cancer in smokers. The effects of genetic susceptibility and vitamin A deficiency on the risk of lung cancer in smokers are unknown, whereas the risk associated with ambient air pollution appears to be small.

Epidemiologic studies have found strong associations between cigarette smoking and the development of cancer at several other sites (e.g., oral cavity, larynx, esophagus, bladder, kidney, pancreas, stomach, and cervix). In general, the smoking-related risk of developing malignancy at these sites is less than for lung cancer. Notably, smokers are at increased risk for a second smoking-related cancer once they have a tobacco-associated malignancy.

CARDIOVASCULAR DISEASE

Prospective studies from different countries have conclusively shown that male and female smokers are at greater risk of myocardial infection, recurrent heart attacks, and sudden death from coronary heart disease (CHD) than nonsmokers. Smokers have a two- to fourfold increased incidence of CHD and a two- to fourfold greater risk of sudden death than nonsmokers. Mortality from CHD can be predicted by the number of cigarettes smoked per day, the depth of inhalation, the age of smoking onset, and the number of years smoked. Additionally, smoking has been shown to greatly modify the risk for CHD associated with other known risk factors such as hypercholesterolemia and diabetes.

Cigarette smoking produces acute and chronic myocardial changes that directly contribute to the development of CHD and its associated complications. Acutely, smoking may cause myocardial ischemia through an increase in oxygen demand or by reducing blood supply. This latter change may result from smoking-related coronary artery spasm and/or platelet aggregation and adhesiveness. Furthermore, smoking can lower the threshold for dysrhythmia, especially ventricular fibrillation, leading to sudden death. Chronically, cigarette smoking can result in coronary atherosclerosis, possibly by causing repetitive endothelial injury; increased platelet adherence with stimulation of smooth muscle proliferation; and increased low-density lipoprotein cholesterol and/or reduced high-density lipoprotein cholesterol.

Several major studies have shown that smoking causes stroke in both men and women. Cigarette smokers have almost a two-fold greater risk of stroke than nonsmokers. This risk is dose-dependent and strongest in younger groups.

SMOKING AND PREGNANCY

Maternal smoking during pregnancy is responsible for a number of significant health risks to the unborn child. Studies over several decades around the world have consistently demonstrated that infants born to mothers who smoke during pregnancy are on average 200 grams lighter and 1 centimeter shorter than infants of nonsmoking mothers. Smoking-related fetal intrauterine growth retardation is a major health concern because it is associated with increased perinatal mortality from a variety of causes. Additionally, women who smoke at the time of conception or during pregnancy are more likely to have spontaneous abortions and pregnancy complications of placenta previa, placental abruption, and premature rupture of membranes than nonsmoking women.

Many of the carcinogenic and mutagenic constituents of tobacco smoke found in the blood of active smokers readily cross the placenta to the fetal circulation. However, the degree to which most of the more than 4000 compounds present in tobacco smoke cross the placenta and the specific compounds that cause adverse health effects on the developing fetus are largely unknown. Nonetheless, the risk of several major birth defects is higher among infants exposed to maternal prenatal smoking,

Recent studies have documented residual development consequences of maternal smoking in pregnancy. In utero exposure of the infant to active maternal smoking has been associated with deficits in lung function, an increased risk of wheezing respiratory illness in early infancy, impairment of somatic (height) growth in childhood, and small deficits in intelligence and behavior as measured on standardized tests. For some of these adverse outcomes, the relative contributions of maternal smoking in pregnancy and in early infancy have not been fully elucidated. . . .

THE ROLE OF ADDICTION

It is well established that nicotine meets the criteria of a highly addictive drug. Like other psychoactive drugs (e.g., cocaine, heroin, or alcohol), nicotine serves as a reinforcer of its use and meets criteria for abuse liability in humans. The nicotine withdrawal syndrome, which is now well characterized, includes craving to use nicotine, irritability, anxiety, difficulty concentrating, restlessness, and increased appetite. Addictions are governed by behavioral, psychological, and biological processes. The fact that smoking has a biologically addictive component does not obviate educational, social, and policy strategies to prevent its onset and promote cessation. . . .

The Health Benefits of Quitting

Smoking cessation has major and immediate health benefits for men and women of all ages. People who quit smoking before age 50 have one-half the risk of dying over the next 15 years compared to people who continue to smoke. This improvement is directly related to specific smoking-related diseases. After 1 year of smoking cessation, the excess risk of CHD mortality is reduced by about one-half and continues to decline with time. Smoking cessation also decreases other nonmalignant disease morbidity and mortality, including that from stroke, peripheral vascular disease, chronic obstructive pulmonary disease (COPD), pneumonia, and gastric or duodenal ulcers. The risk of lung cancer declines steadily in people who quit smoking until, after 10 years, the risk is about 30 to 50% of that in continuing smokers. Smoking cessation also reduced the risk of other tobacco-related malignancies, including cancers of the larynx, esophagus, pancreas, and urinary bladder. The health benefits of smoking cessation are immediate and substantial, extending to men and women of all ages, both sick and healthy. . . .

Cigarette smoking remains the primary cause of preventable death and morbidity in the United States. Smoking causes lung cancer, COPD, and CHD and contributes significantly to mortality from other conditions such as stroke. Maternal smoking during pregnancy causes low birthweight and perinatal mortality, and it may have lasting impact on the child's physical and cognitive growth. Passive exposure to environmental tobacco smoke (ETS) causes lung cancer and poses particular danger to the respiratory health of young children. Smoking cessation strategies are important, but they should be supplemented by community and policy-level interventions. Workplace or community smoking bans, statewide taxes on tobacco, and antismoking media campaigns may be effective adjuncts to individual cessation strategies. These strategies may be an even more important disincentive to smoking initiation. The expanding horizon of health consequences of smoking and its costs to American society should again challenge public health agencies to develop and implement effective strategies to prevent smoking acquisition by young people. These health effects should also motivate health professionals in other countries where smoking prevalence is increasing, rather than decreasing, to initiate more effective efforts to reverse this trend and minimize the excess morbidity and death that accompany this dangerous habit.

"Beware of the massive campaign
being launched that seeks to blame
every ill known to man on cigarette
smoking."

THE HARMFUL EFFECTS OF CIGARETTE SMOKING ARE EXAGGERATED

Part I: Rosalind B. Marimont; Part II: Charley Reese

The authors of the following two-part viewpoint maintain that the health risks attributed to smoking have been exaggerated. In Part I, Rosalind B. Marimont contends that the government's faulty reports on the dangers of smoking have confused and misguided the public. Marimont is a retired mathematician and scientist who is active in health policy issues. In Part II, syndicated columnist Charley Reese claims that the American government and corporations have overstated the dangers of smoking to deflect attention from the health problems caused by industrial pollution.

As you read, consider the following questions:

1. What is wrong with the claim that smoking kills four hundred thousand Americans annually, according to Marimont?
2. According to Marimont, what are some of the health benefits of smoking cigarettes?
3. How do the death rates from lung cancer compare with the death rates from pneumonia and influenza, according to Reese?

Part I: Reprinted from "Casualties of the War on Smoking," by Rosalind B. Marimont, on the FORCES USA website (www.forces.org/pages/roz-03.htm), July 10, 1997, by permission of the author. Part II: From "Blowing Smoke in People's Eyes," by Charley Reese, syndicated column of January 29, 1993, at www.smokers.org/research/articles/07-blowing_smoke. html. Reprinted by special permission from King Features Syndicate.

I

In the War on Smoking, truth has been the first casualty. Junk science has replaced honest science, and propaganda parades as fact. By vastly overrating the dangers of tobacco, and neglecting those of alcohol and drugs, the Anti-Smoking Partisans (ASPs) have gravely distorted the proper priorities for our resources.

FAULTY INFORMATION ABOUT SMOKING

Americans now accept as gospel in the Holy War on Smoking many statements that are not true. For example:

• *It is false that smoking kills 400,000 Americans annually.* This Centers for Disease Control (CDC) number is nothing but an estimate generated by a computer program called SAMMEC, based on an erroneous model, ignoring all the rules of epidemiology, and vastly inflating the effects of smoking. For example, if Joe Smith is obese, has high cholesterol, diabetes, a family history of heart attacks, never exercises, smokes, and dies of a heart attack, the CDC attributes his death to smoking only! SAMMEC is also the basis for other scare numbers, such as that 3 million or 5 million of today's children will die from smoking.

• *It is false that smoking is a major danger to children.* Children do not die of tobacco-related diseases. If they smoke heavily they may die of lung cancer in their old age, 50 years from now, if lung cancer is still a threat. But now and this year they are dying by the thousands in accidents, suicides, and homicides, largely associated with drugs and alcohol. It is unconscionable to keep diverting resources to the far future tobacco threat and ignore the immediate drug and alcohol threat, which can kill children long before they can get cancer!

• *It is false that secondhand smoke (ETS) is a proven health danger.* The Environmental Protection Agency (EPA) report naming ETS as a Class A carcinogen is a triumph of politics over science, and a symbol of corruption of science by government. The Congressional Research Service (CRS) of the Library of Congress, in a perfectly clear but discreetly worded report, showed that objective evaluation of the evidence did not support the EPA contention that ETS is a major health hazard.

EXAGGERATING THE DANGERS OF SMOKING

• *It is false that tobacco is more dangerous than drugs or alcohol.* The CDC inflates the deaths from tobacco, and ignores the fact that tobacco is not an intoxicant, and alcohol and drugs are. Intoxicants destroy physical coordination, emotional restraint, and moral standards. Alcohol and drug abuse contribute to crime, violence, spouse abuse, child neglect, sexual promiscuity and sexually transmitted diseases. Nicotine does none of these things.

• *It is false that smokers are a financial burden to society.* Economists, with rare unanimity, have shown that smokers are not a net cost to the government, but a saving. Smokers pay heavy cigarette taxes, and also, because their life expectancy is somewhat less than non-smokers (by about 3 to five years), they collect less in Social Security, pensions, Medicare, and Medicaid. A complete report on these economic matters was issued by the Congressional Research Service of the Library of Congress in March 1994.

• *It is false that smoking has no health benefits at all.* Smokers are less obese than non-smokers, and since obesity is a risk factor for heart disease, diabetes, and stroke, preventing obesity should count as a benefit in health reckoning. Nicotine also has an antidepressant, anti-anxiety effect, improves alertness, attention, and concentration. There is increasing evidence that smoking tends to reduce the risk of Alzheimer's and Parkinson's diseases, and to ameliorate the symptoms of schizophrenia. Scientists in these fields have a great deal of trouble getting funding, because ASPs, who control federal money, cannot admit that smoking has any benefits.

The ASPs have managed to convince the American people that all these falsehoods are true. They used the Big Lie Technique, a favorite of Hitler, who knew that people will believe anything if leaders repeat it often enough.

What are the true effects of this propaganda masterstroke?

The Corrupting of Science

ASPs dominate the Federal Health Establishment, particularly since the Clintons took over the White House. Federal money, the chief support for most health scientists, has been used to produce mountains of pseudo-statistics, which laypeople can't understand, and "experts" can easily use. The Centers for Disease Control (CDC) and the Environmental Protection Agency (EPA) produce junk science faster than honest scientists can debunk it. Worst of all, ASPs mercilessly suppress criticism by honest scientists, whom they vilify as dishonest tools of the tobacco companies.

Theodor Sterling, a fellow of the American College of Epidemiology, wrote a tongue-in-cheek piece showing that the CDC method could be used to prove that *not smoking* caused 270,000 deaths a year. He wrote a serious paper showing that by use of only 2 honest corrections to the CDC work, the number of purported smoking deaths could be cut in half. Sterling was blasted by the ASP guru Stanton Glantz, whose economic work has recently been demolished by the economist Michael Evans.

The Federal Health Establishment, controlling a vast portion of biomedical research money, has the power to deny grants and end the careers of scientists critical of ASP dogma. In fact, censorship has gone so far that many American journals will not publish or even review papers by authors who receive any money from tobacco interests! . . .

"I THINK THIS ANTI-TOBACCO SENTIMENT HAS GONE TO OVERKILL"

Dave Catrow. Reprinted by permission of Copley News Service.

The War on Smoking, which started with a germ of truth—that smoking is a high risk factor for lung cancer—has grown into a monster of deceit, tyranny, and greed, further eroding the credibility of the government, and harming our health and welfare. The true dangers to our society are crime, violence, family breakdown, and out-of-wedlock births. None of these arises from smoking, but from alcohol and drug abuse, lack of moral values, and poverty.

II

Okay. Okay. If you smoke, quit. If you don't, don't start. It's probably not healthy.

Now, with that out of the way, beware of the massive campaign being launched that seeks to blame every ill known to man on cigarette smoking.

It smells strongly of a disinformation campaign, of a campaign to use the cigarette as a diversion or a "fall weed," so to speak.

POLLUTION AND PROPAGANDA

I'm not talking about the happy hysterics who believe everything they read in a newspaper or hear on television. They're the same people who enrich TV sitcom producers. I'm not talking about the militantly self-righteous former addicts. I'm not talking about the neurotic egotists who think even a squirrel breaking wind is a capital offense against their unrestricted right to atmospheric nirvana.

No, I'm really talking about the chemical, herbicide, pesticide, petro-chemical industries who are loathe for anyone to suggest that the massive tonnage of airborne pollution could possibly cause anyone the slightest health problem. Obviously, it doesn't. Cigarettes are to blame.

One Establishment columnist recently drew a specious parallel between the rise of cigarette production at the turn of the twentieth century and the rise of lung cancer death rates. Why specious?

Well, because many other things occurred since the turn of the twentieth century besides the production of cigarettes. How about, for example, urbanization by which 70 percent of the population concentrated itself in cities where probably 80 percent of the motor vehicles are concentrated. At the turn of the twentieth century only 4,000 cars were sold in the U.S. In 1992 over 10 million were sold. Today, approximately 183 million automobiles and trucks defile the air in the U.S. One car in a half block of travel produces more carbon monoxide than multiple packs of cigarettes.

In 1989, for example, we happily consumed 6.3 billion barrels of oil. Altogether, we consumed 81.28 quadrillion BTUs of energy. Keep in mind that old law in physics that nothing is destroyed. When you burn one gallon of fuel, it doesn't disappear—it just changes form and part of it comes out the tailpipe or the smokestack.

In 1989, sales of industrial chemicals and allied products added up to $67 billion. Lead production was over 300,000 metric tons. The use of pesticides and herbicides, both in agriculture and in and around homes, has mushroomed tremendously in this century.

A DISINFORMATION CAMPAIGN

So what does it all mean? I'll spell it out. I'm suggesting that one reason at least for the inordinate amount of propaganda about cigarettes is to divert attention from the health effects of industrial pollution. The government—and the Fortune 500 crowd—shy away from that subject like a horse from a rattlesnake.

Blame it all on cigarettes. It's a lot cheaper—from their standpoint.

Unfortunately for the propaganda, the death rate for lung cancer after all these billions of cigarettes is only 20 per hundred thousand, which compares to 29.8 per hundred thousand for pneumonia and influenza and 37.2 per hundred thousand for accidents.

Not to worry, the anti-smoker crowd blames everything, most especially heart disease, on smoking, as if diet, stress, exercise and genes had nothing to do with it. One wonders why so many health food fanatics and fitness and wellness gurus who have never smoked keep dropping dead from heart attacks.

Now, for the nerds who can't read simple English, let me recapitulate. I am not saying smoking cigarettes is healthy. I am not saying smoking may not be a factor in cancer and heart disease. I am saying that the propaganda being directed at tobacco is suspiciously out of proportion and often specious, often based on faulty studies.

I am saying you ought to ask yourself why this is so.

| "The presence of nicotine in tobacco products makes them addictive and is the reason many people smoke."

NICOTINE IS ADDICTIVE

Clifford E. Douglas

Clifford E. Douglas is a government relations consultant to the American Cancer Society in Washington, D.C. In the following viewpoint, excerpted from a report written for the American Council on Science and Health, Douglas argues that the nicotine found in cigarettes and other tobacco products makes them highly addictive. He contends, moreover, that tobacco manufacturers are aware of nicotine's addictiveness and deliberately boost the chemical's content in cigarettes; because of this, Douglas claims, many people habitually smoke even when they are aware of tobacco's dangers.

As you read, consider the following questions:

1. What are some of the chemicals found in cigarette smoke, according to Douglas?
2. According to the author, why have cigarettes and other tobacco products not been regulated by the Food and Drug Administration?
3. In Douglas's opinion, what evidence reveals the tobacco industry's awareness of nicotine's addictiveness?

Reprinted, with permission, from Clifford E. Douglas, "The Tobacco Industry's Use of Nicotine as a Drug," a (May 1994) publication of the American Council on Science and Health, 1995 Broadway, 2nd Floor, New York, NY 10023-5860.

On February 28, 1994, *Day One*, a magazine show produced by ABC News, aired an exposé on the tobacco industry's manipulation of nicotine. The segment, and a follow-up segment which aired on March 7, 1994, resulted from a year-long investigation by Pulitzer Prize-winning journalist Walt Bogdanich, a *Day One* producer and former *Wall Street Journal* reporter, and associate producer Keith Summa. The imminent airing of the first segment on a Monday prompted the release the preceding Friday of a remarkable letter by Food and Drug Administration (FDA) Commissioner David Kessler announcing that in light of the new evidence the FDA would consider regulating tobacco products as drugs. While the FDA reportedly had been interested for some time in pursuing regulatory action against tobacco products, the information obtained by *Day One* provided the "hook" the FDA needed in order to proceed.

The evidence uncovered by *Day One* and assembled by FDA investigators illustrates publicly for the first time the extent to which the tobacco industry is capable of and does in fact manipulate the amount and even the presence of nicotine in cigarettes. Before these recent revelations, nicotine generally was perceived to be merely a natural part of the tobacco leaf and an inevitable component of any tobacco product. The potential implication of the new disclosures is substantial.

After four years of independently investigating the subject of nicotine manipulation, I pitched the story to ABC in the fall of 1992 and assisted *Day One* during its investigation. The information and insights offered in this viewpoint come, in part, from this experience. . . .

TOBACCO PRODUCTS ARE ADDICTIVE

The presence of nicotine in tobacco products makes them addictive and is the reason many people smoke despite the evidence of the deadly effects of tobacco use.

Nicotine appears naturally in tobacco and is absorbed into the body when tobacco is smoked, chewed or sniffed. Nicotine has always been perceived as an inevitable part of the tobacco products. "If you used tobacco, you ingested nicotine."

The role of nicotine in tobacco products has been studied for years. In the early 1980's, a scientific consensus developed that cigarettes are not just habit-forming but addictive in the same way that drugs such as cocaine and heroin are addictive. This research resulted in an entire report by the U.S. Surgeon General devoted to the addictive nature of tobacco products and the central role that nicotine plays in causing that addiction. The release of the 1988 Surgeon General's report silenced any lingering, credible scientific debate about whether tobacco products are addictive and whether nicotine is the substance in tobacco products that makes them addictive. The latest Surgeon General's report on children and tobacco, issued on February 24, 1994, confirmed that the nicotine in tobacco products is responsible for the rapid addiction of up to half of all children who experiment with tobacco.

THE POISONS IN CIGARETTE SMOKE

Nicotine's impact on tobacco usage and the resulting epidemic of tobacco-related disease was examined in a 1991 editorial in the *Lancet*:

> The core of the problem lies in the addictiveness of nicotine. It is nicotine that people cannot easily do without, not tobacco; it is nicotine dependence that slows the progress of existing programmes. As a drug delivery system the modern cigarette is a highly efficient device for getting nicotine to the brain, but by pharmaceutical standards it is also a very dirty one, the nicotine being contaminated with nitrosamines and other carcinogens in the tar, as well as with carbon monoxide and other harmful gases.

Cigarette smoke contains such chemicals as arsenic (poison), ammonia (toilet cleaner), carbon monoxide (car exhaust fumes), methane (swamp gas), acetone (nail polish remover) and formaldehyde (used to preserve dead bodies), among thousands of others, and would remain a serious health risk in the absence of nicotine. In other words, taking nicotine out of cigarettes would not make them safe. However, few people would use nonaddictive tobacco products, and thus few would subsequently face exposure to these other harmful chemicals. Furthermore, new smokers, mainly adolescents, would not become addicted in the first place.

FDA REGULATIONS

The FDA regulates nicotine when included in other products but has declined to regulate it in tobacco products. (Favor, a nicotine delivery system produced by Advanced Tobacco Products, was somewhat an exception to this rule. It was regulated by the FDA on the basis of its nicotine content.)

Federal law gives the FDA regulatory authority over food, drugs and cosmetics. Tobacco products (cigarettes, chewing tobacco, snuff, etc.) are not considered foods under the law. Nor have they been considered as drugs, as defined by the FDA. To conclude that a product is a drug, the FDA has held that the product must not only affect the structure and function of the body; in addition, the seller (manufacturer) must intend it to do so. Thus, [prior to 1996] the FDA determined that cigarettes which are advertised and sold "for smoking pleasure only" were not drugs.

NICOTINE ADDICTION

As with dependence on other drugs, cigarette smoking tends to be a progressive, chronic, relapsing disorder. The most notable distinction between cigarette smoking and other drug dependencies is that a much higher percentage of people who start smoking escalate and graduate to dependent levels than with other addictive drugs. About 1 in 10 smokers in this country is a low-level smoker, termed a "chipper," who smokes 5 or fewer cigarettes per day; most of the rest show evidence of dependence. This is in contrast to alcohol use, where 10 to 15 percent of alcohol drinkers are problem drinkers; the rest generally drink in moderation and at times of their own choosing.

People do not start smoking a pack of cigarettes per day. They likely would become ill at that level of nicotine intake. Rather, they start out with low levels. Over months and years, most people progress to higher and higher nicotine intake. They become tolerant; that is, nicotine loses effectiveness with its continued presence in the body, and it is necessary to increase the dose to maintain its effectiveness after repeated administrations. Eventually, smokers do more than simply tolerate high nicotine doses; they need continued nicotine to feel normal and function satisfactorily. At this point, smokers may go to great lengths to continue smoking and sustain their nicotine intake within upper and lower boundaries so that their intake does not fall low enough that they experience withdrawal symptoms or high enough to produce adverse effects.

Jack E. Henningfield and Leslie M. Schuh, *Smoking and Tobacco Control Monograph No. 7*, 1997.

Even so, the FDA has long recognized nicotine as both an addictive and toxic substance. Thus, the agency tightly regulates the sale and use of nicotine in all forms and in all products (i.e., nicotine gum or nicotine patches) except when sold for "pleasure" as part of a tobacco product. Until now, the FDA's rationale for not regulating nicotine when sold as part of a tobacco product has been that there is inadequate evidence that nicotine in tobacco products is sold with the intent to have a pharmacologic effect on the body. [In 1996, the FDA determined that the nicotine in cigarettes and smokeless tobacco is a drug.]

The tobacco industry knows that nicotine is addictive.

Internal tobacco industry documents made public during the trial in *Cipollone v. Liggett* in the 1980's demonstrate the industry's understanding of the central role that nicotine plays in causing and sustaining addiction. For example, an internal report written in 1972 by William L. Dunn, Jr., a senior scientist with the Philip Morris Tobacco Company, says the following:

> As with eating and copulating, so it is with smoking. The physiological effect serves as the primary incentive; all other incentives are secondary. . . . Without nicotine, the argument goes, there would be no smoking. Some strong evidence can be marshaled to support this argument: (1) No one has ever become a cigarette smoker by smoking cigarettes without nicotine. (2) Most of the physiological responses to inhaled smoke have been shown to be nicotine-related.

> Why then is there not a market for nicotine per se, to be eaten, sucked, drunk, injected, inserted or inhaled as a pure aerosol? The answer, and I feel quite strongly about this, is that the cigarette is in fact among the most awe-inspiring examples of the ingenuity of man. . . .

> The cigarette should be conceived not as a product but as a package. The product is nicotine. The cigarette is but one of many package layers. There is the carton, which contains the pack, which contains the cigarette, which contains the smoke. The smoke is the final package. The smoker must strip off all these package layers to get to that which he seeks. . . .

> Think of the cigarette pack as a storage container for [a] day's supply of nicotine. . . . Think of the cigarette as a dispenser for a dose unit of nicotine. . . . Think of a puff of smoke as the vehicle of nicotine. . . . Smoke is beyond question the most optimized vehicle of nicotine and the cigarette the most optimized dispenser of smoke.

DESTROYING EVIDENCE OF NICOTINE'S DANGERS

Moreover, it was not disclosed until March 1994 that Philip Morris's own researchers prepared a paper in 1983—five years before the Surgeon General's landmark report on addiction—reporting that they had found nicotine to be addictive in rats. The report was peer reviewed and accepted for publication in a respected scientific publication, *Psychopharmacology*, but then withdrawn on the company's orders. Subsequently, Philip Morris closed the researchers' laboratory and destroyed evidence of their work.

In their defense, the major cigarette manufacturers have argued of late that their products contain less nicotine now than they did in the 1950's. This appears to be false. In 1952, the FDA found that the tobacco from the five leading cigarette brands contained an average of 1.58–1.82 percent nicotine on a dry weight basis. This was less nicotine than the 1.5–2.5 percent nicotine reported for finished cigarettes by R.J. Reynolds Tobacco's (RJR's) chief executive James Johnston in a March 1994 letter to the FDA. . . .

THE MANIPULATION OF NICOTINE CONTENT

While it has been known for some time that tobacco manufacturers have some control over nicotine, the new evidence shows that:

• Tobacco manufacturers have the capability to remove all or virtually all of the nicotine from their tobacco products using technology already in existence.

• They currently remove substantial quantities of the nicotine from tobacco, manipulate it and then apply it to the final manufactured product in carefully controlled, precisely measured quantities. According to experts in the tobacco manufacturing process, leading cigarette brands contain a significant percentage of nicotine that was previously extracted from tobacco, manipulated and reapplied. A lawyer for RJR testified before Congress in 1988 that approximately 70 percent of the nicotine contained in the company's ill-fated nicotine delivery device, Premier (which some observers inaccurately dubbed a "smokeless cigarette"), consisted of separately added nicotine extract.

• Tobacco manufacturers add substantial quantities of nicotine to their products that they have purchased from other sources, including firms which specialize in extracting and processing nicotine and other substances.

In a nutshell, what this means is that while nicotine appears naturally in raw tobacco, it is no longer an unavoidable component of a tobacco product. Today, tobacco manufacturers consciously manipulate nicotine during the manufacturing process. They add nicotine to the processed tobacco and other contents of the manufactured product.

While manufacturers have used a number of euphemisms to describe the role of nicotine, there is widespread agreement in the medical and scientific communities that its primary, if not sole, function is to make the product addictive.

> "If nicotine is *so* relentlessly
> addictive, how can it be that 50
> percent of all Americans who have
> ever smoked no longer do?"

NICOTINE IS NOT NECESSARILY ADDICTIVE

Richard J. DeGrandpre

Nicotine cannot be exclusively blamed for addiction to cigarettes, asserts Richard J. DeGrandpre in the following viewpoint. According to DeGrandpre, people may acquire a cigarette smoking habit not due to a physical dependence on nicotine but due to psychological or social reasons. A fuller understanding of the process of addiction is needed to help curb cigarette addiction, he concludes. DeGrandpre, an independent scholar of drugs and culture, is coeditor of *Drug Policy and Human Nature* and coauthor of *The Changing Self.*

As you read, consider the following questions:

1. What are the claims of the classical model of addiction, according to DeGrandpre?
2. In what way is cigarette addiction a psychosocial process, according to the author?
3. What are the three levels of complexity seen in the addiction process, in DeGrandpre's opinion?

During the 1996 presidential election campaign, Bill Clinton successfully cast Big Tobacco as a national enemy, with Bob Dole playing the role of collaborator by downplaying the addictiveness of nicotine. Meanwhile, the Food and Drug Administration has been asserting jurisdiction over cigarettes as "nicotine delivery devices," arguing that tobacco companies intend to hook their customers, just like schoolyard drug pushers. Hundreds of pending lawsuits, including class actions and cases filed by state governments, similarly allege a conspiracy to addict smokers. These developments represent important changes in our attitudes toward cigarettes. Though justified in the name of public health, the increasing emphasis on the enslaving power of nicotine may only make matters worse.

THE CLASSICAL MODEL OF ADDICTION

Understanding why requires careful consideration of the conventional wisdom about tobacco addiction, which recycles mistaken assumptions about illicit drugs. During the latter half of this century, the classical model of addiction, derived from observations of narcotic abuse, increasingly has been used to describe the cigarette habit. The classical model states that consumption of certain chemicals causes a physical dependence, either immediately or after prolonged use, characterized by withdrawal symptoms—symptoms that can be avoided or escaped only by further drug use. As Steven Hyman, director of the National Institute of Mental Health (NIMH), opined recently in *Science*, "Repeated doses of addictive drugs—opiates, cocaine, and amphetamine—cause drug dependence and, afterward, withdrawal."

This cyclical model, in which the drug serves as both problem and solution, offers a simple, easy-to-grasp account of the addiction process, giving the concept great staying power in the public imagination. In the case of smoking, this view of addiction is central to the rationale for regulating tobacco and the concern that the cigarette companies have been doping their products with extra nicotine. But the classical model tends to conceal rather than elucidate the ultimate sources of addiction, and it is just as ill-suited to the cigarette habit as it has always been for understanding illicit drug use.

If a chemical compound can be addictive in the manner described by NIMH Director Hyman, we would expect anyone who regularly uses such a substance to become addicted. Yet only a minority of those who use illicit drugs—whether marijuana, cocaine, or heroin—ever develop a dependence on them.

The prevalence of addiction, as defined by the American Psychiatric Association's *Diagnostic and Statistical Manual*, among users of alcohol and cocaine runs about 15 percent and 17 percent, respectively. Even in a sample of 79 regular crack users, Patricia Erickson and her colleagues at Toronto's Addiction Research Foundation found that only about 37 percent used the drug heavily (more than 100 times in their lives), and 67 percent had not used in the past month. A similar pattern holds for tobacco. In the 1994 National Household Survey on Drug Abuse, 73 percent of respondents reported smoking cigarettes at some time, but only about 29 percent reported smoking in the previous month, and not necessarily on a daily basis. Writing in the May/June 1996 *Mother Jones*, Jeffrey Klein manages to argue that nicotine enslaves its users and, at the same time, that Tobacco Inc. seeks to recruit young smokers to replace the 1.3 million Americans who quit each year. If nicotine is so relentlessly addictive, how can it be that 50 percent of all Americans who have ever smoked no longer do?

CIGARETTE ADDICTION OR NICOTINE ADDICTION?

The classical model also suggests that the cigarette habit should be highly amenable to nicotine replacement therapy, such as the nicotine patch. Yet few of the tens of thousands of patch users have actually broken the habit (only about 10 percent to 15 percent succeed). In direct conflict with the classical model, most keep smoking while on the patch, continuing to consume the carcinogens in cigarette smoke while obtaining considerably higher blood levels of nicotine. A 1992 study of nicotine replacement therapy reported in the journal *Psychopharmacology* concluded that the "overall lack of effect [of the patch] on cigarette consumption is perhaps surprising and suggests that in regular smokers the lighting up of a cigarette is generally triggered by cues other than low plasma nicotine levels."

Most people who successfully quit smoking do so only after several failed attempts. If addiction is driven by physical dependence on a chemical—in this case, nicotine—relapse should occur during withdrawal, which for nicotine typically lasts a few weeks. Yet a sizable proportion of relapses occur long after the smoker has suffered through nicotine withdrawal. In fact, studies do not even show a relationship between the severity of withdrawal and the likelihood of relapse. As any former smoker could tell you, ex-smokers crave cigarettes at certain times and in certain situations for months, even years, after quitting. In these cases, the desire to smoke is triggered by environmental cues, not by withdrawal symptoms. This is one reason why people who overcome addiction to illicit substances such as heroin or cocaine often say they had more difficulty breaking the cigarette habit. Because regular tobacco users smoke in a wide array of circumstances (when bored, after eating, when driving) and settings (home, work, car), the cues that elicit the urge are more ubiquitous than for illicit drug use.

Smokers Are Not Drug Addicts

[Some contend] that nicotine is an addictive drug and that, therefore, smokers are drug addicts. I object to the premise and to the conclusion.

Many people like to smoke. Some people like the look and feel of the pack or the smell of tobacco. Some like to hold and fiddle with a cigarette. And, of course, there is the taste and aroma of the tobacco, and the sight of the smoke.

Cigarettes contain nicotine because it occurs naturally in tobacco. Nicotine contributes to the taste of cigarettes and the pleasure of smoking. The presence of nicotine, however, does not make cigarettes a drug or smoking an addiction.

William I. Campbell, statement before the House Committee on Energy and Commerce, Subcommittee on Health and the Environment, April 14, 1994.

These failures of the classical model illustrate how conventional wisdom oversimplifies the dynamics of cigarette smoking. This reductionist view is dangerous because it ignores the psychosocial factors that underlie addiction. In coming to terms with cigarette addiction as a psychosocial process, rather than a simple pharmacological one, we need to distinguish between cigarette addiction and nicotine addiction. Certainly no one (except perhaps the tobacco companies) denies that cigarette smoking can be addictive, if by addiction one means a stubborn urge to keep smoking. But it is quite a different matter to say that nicotine accounts for the addictiveness of smoking. Nicotine withdrawal notwithstanding, nicotine alone is insufficient, and may even be unnecessary, to create cigarette addiction.

Addictions Are Not Always Drug Related

This claim can be clarified by two dramatic case studies reported in the *British Journal of Addiction* in 1973 and 1989. The earlier article described a 47-year-old woman with a two-and-a-half-year-long dependence on *water*, one of several such cases noted by the author. The woman reported a nagging withdrawal symptom—a dry, salty taste in her mouth—that was alleviated by the persistent drinking of water (up to 60 glasses per day). This case of dependence on a nonpsychoactive substance contrasts sharply with the second account, which described an 80-year-old woman who used cocaine without incident for 55 years. The authors reported that "she denies any feelings of euphoria or increased energy after [snorting] the cocaine nor any depression or craving for cocaine when her supplies run out. . . . She appears to have suffered no ill effects from the prolonged use of cocaine in physical, psychological or social terms." So we see that not every addiction involves drug use and not every instance of drug use involves an addiction.

To say that cigarette addiction is a psychosocial process means that social, cultural, and economic factors play a crucial role in acquiring and keeping a cigarette habit. In fact, the tendency to reduce the cigarette experience to chemical servitude may be one of the most powerful cultural factors driving addiction. Cigarette lore wrongly teaches smokers (and smokers-to-be) that they will suffer badly if they attempt to quit, while at the same time freeing them of responsibility for their drug use once they begin. Such beliefs also help romanticize cigarette smoking, elevating nicotine to a sublime abstraction. This not only reinforces the forbidden fruit effect, it helps transform the habit of smoking into a cult behavior. Smoking thus acquires the kind of meaning that the youth of America are most in search of: social meaning. As Richard Klein writes in *Cigarettes Are Sublime*, "smoking cigarettes is not only a physical act but a discursive one—a wordless but eloquent form of expression."

UNDERSTANDING THE ADDICTION PROCESS

To counteract the forces that give momentum to drug use, the public meaning of addiction needs to be broadened to include the many, changing facets of the psychosocial realm in which we develop. "Putting people back in charge" of their addictions, as John Leo puts it in *U.S. News & World Report*, will not work if we focus only on the naked individual. Rather than pushing the pendulum of public policy between scapegoating the substance and scapegoating the individual, we should seek a middle ground. Realizing that the addiction process has at least three levels of complexity is a good place to start.

First, at the basic and most immediate level, are the short- and long-term biological processes that underlie the psychological experiences of drug use and drug abstinence. Even with the same drug, these experiences vary greatly across individuals. Scientists and journalists too easily forget that every psychological process is built on biology. Discoveries of biological mechanisms and processes underlying addiction are not proof that the problem is biological rather than social and psychological. Eating rich foods has powerful biological effects in both the short and long run, but we should not therefore conclude that the rise in obesity in the United States is a biological problem. Indeed, attempts to alter the addiction process that emphasize biochemistry (such as the nicotine patch) have met with little success.

At the next level are psychological processes (social, motivational, learning) that, although rooted in biology, are shaped by personal experience. Because each of us has unique life experiences, we do not necessarily interpret the same events in the same way. The reasons for one individual's addiction may be altogether different from the reasons for another's. As the 1996 Scottish film *Trainspotting* makes clear, stories of addiction are no less complex than any other personal stories. Still, intervention at this level has had some success with users of alcohol or illicit drugs, and several research and treatment institutions are examining methods for "matching" addicts with different treatment strategies based on their social and psychological characteristics.

Drug effects and drug addiction also vary greatly across time and place, implicating cultural factors as the third and most general aspect of drug addiction. These factors are rooted in but not reducible to psychological processes, just as psychological processes are not reducible to biology. Patterns of alcohol use around the world, which show that the prevalence of drinking problems cannot be predicted by consumption alone, illustrate the importance of culture. Italians, for example, historically have consumed large quantities of alcohol with relatively low rates of drunkenness and alcoholism. The effects of alcohol on human behavior—violence, boorishness, gregariousness—also have been shown to vary dramatically across cultures.

Given the cultural role in addiction and the radical changes that have occurred in attitudes about smoking, it is quite possible that the young smokers of today are not at all like the smokers of 50 years ago. Those who begin smoking now do so with the belief that it is addictive, causes poor health (and wrinkles!), and can be deadly. If individuals are willing to start smoking despite such knowledge, it is likely that they will acquire and keep the habit, seeming to confirm the current, politically correct image of addiction. And if this self-fulfilling prophecy is realized, chances are that interventions aimed at the social realm will continue to miss their target and fail to curtail addiction.

> "Environmental tobacco smoke . . . is estimated to cause 53,000 deaths each year among nonsmokers in the United States."

SECONDHAND SMOKE IS HARMFUL

John R. Garrison

In the following viewpoint, John R. Garrison argues that exposure to environmental tobacco smoke—secondhand smoke—is harmful to the health of nonsmokers. According to Garrison, secondhand smoke causes lung cancer, increases the risk of heart disease, and adversely affects the health of youths and unborn children. He contends that stronger restrictions on smoking in public places would help protect Americans from the dangers of secondhand smoke. Garrison is the managing director of the American Lung Association.

As you read, consider the following questions:

1. According to the EPA, how many lung cancer deaths are caused by secondhand smoke each year?
2. According to the author, secondhand smoke increases the risk for what kinds of respiratory problems in infants and young children?
3. What restrictions have been placed on smoking in public places, according to Garrison?

The toxic effects of secondhand smoke have been so well-documented during the last 25 years that there should be no doubt that smoke emitted from other people's cigarettes is a real and preventable health risk. Secondhand smoke, also known as environmental tobacco smoke, or ETS, passive smoke or sidestream smoke is estimated to cause 53,000 deaths each year among nonsmokers in the United States. The Environmental Protection Agency, or EPA, estimates that secondhand smoke is responsible for about 3,000 lung-cancer deaths each year among nonsmokers; of these, an estimated 800 are due to exposure to secondhand smoke in the home and 2,200 from exposure at work or in social settings. A recent study from Harvard University reports that ETS may even double a person's risk of heart disease.

THE THREAT OF SECONDHAND SMOKE

Unlike the dangers of cigarette use, the threat that secondhand smoke presents is especially insidious because it affects the health of adults and children who cannot always protect themselves: Children do not choose to live in smoke-filled homes, and nonsmoking adults can't control the smoky air they breathe at work.

The scientific community began compiling evidence about the adverse health effects of secondhand smoke as early as 1972, when a report of the surgeon general concluded that "an atmosphere contaminated with tobacco smoke can contribute to the discomfort of many individuals."

Since then, several reports have been released outlining the toxic effects of secondhand smoke. They include the 1986 surgeon general's report which concluded that secondhand smoke can cause lung cancer in healthy nonsmokers and that children whose parents smoke have an increased frequency of respiratory infections and respiratory symptoms compared with children whose parents do not smoke. The National Academy of Sciences and the International Agency for Research on Cancer also issued reports in 1986 that offered similar conclusions.

In 1991, the National Institute for Occupational Safety and Health, or NIOSH, concluded that ETS is a potential occupational carcinogen. NIOSH recommended that employers take measures to reduce their employees' exposure to secondhand smoke by designating a separate area for smoking.

THE EPA REPORT

The final breakthrough came in 1993, with the publication of the EPA's definitive report, *Respiratory Health Effects of Passive Smoking:*

Lung Cancer and Other Disorders. This report not only supported earlier findings regarding the risks of lung cancer, it also augmented previous reports with an exhaustive review of the health effects of secondhand smoke on children.

The EPA's report classified secondhand smoke as a Group A carcinogen that is responsible for an estimated annual toll of 37,000 heart-disease deaths and 13,000 deaths from other cancers in U.S. nonsmokers. Secondhand smoke was found to be a risk factor for the development of asthma in children. It also was found to worsen asthma symptoms for up to 1 million children already diagnosed with asthma. Annually, an estimated 150,000 to 300,000 cases of lower-respiratory-tract infections, such as bronchitis and pneumonia, among children under 18 months of age were linked to secondhand smoke exposure. The EPA report also concluded that infants and young children exposed to secondhand smoke experience increased cases of ear infection, coughing, wheezing and mucus buildup.

The EPA report was subjected to an extensive open review both by the public and the agency's Science Advisory Board, a panel of independent scientific experts. The board, the Department of Health and Human Services, the National Cancer Institute, the surgeon general and many other major health organizations, including the American Lung Association, have endorsed the EPA's findings.

SECONDHAND SMOKE CAUSES LUNG CANCER

Despite these endorsements, the tobacco industry continues to question the EPA's conclusions on lung cancer. While the industry neither acknowledges nor disputes the EPA's findings on the respiratory effects in children, it continues to argue that the EPA manipulated the lung-cancer data to arrive at a predetermined conclusion. Furthermore, the tobacco industry argues that a nonsmoker's exposure to secondhand smoke is so minimal as to be insignificant.

The EPA's findings that secondhand smoke exposure causes lung cancer in nonsmoking adults was not based on a single analysis but, rather, on the total weight of all the evidence available at the time. In addition, no claims ever have been made that minimal exposure to secondhand smoke poses a huge individual cancer risk. While the lung-cancer risk from secondhand smoke is relatively small compared with the risk from smoking, exposure to secondhand smoke often is involuntary and varies greatly among exposed individuals. Clearly, those who work or live with smokers experience a greater risk of lung cancer than those who are less exposed.

Several lung cancer studies published since the release of the EPA report reinforce the link between secondhand smoke exposure and lung cancer. They include a 1992 study by Stockwell et al. that found a group of Florida women whose husbands smoked experienced a 60 percent increase of lung cancer risk. A similar study of Missouri women conducted the same year by Brownson et al. found a significant increase in risk among women exposed to high levels of secondhand smoke from their spouses. Finally, a 1994 study by Fontham et al. found significant increases in lung cancer risk among women in two California and three Southern cities who were exposed to secondhand smoke.

THE EFFECTS OF ETS ON CHILDREN

There is no doubt today that smoking by parents is associated with a broad range of adverse effects in children. Tobacco use during pregnancy is responsible for an estimated 20 to 30 percent of low-birthweight babies, up to 14 percent of preterm deliveries and some 10 percent of all infant deaths.

Reprinted by permission of Mike Luckovich and Creators Syndicate.

A study reported by the *American Journal of Respiratory and Critical Care Medicine* in 1992 found that even apparently healthy, full-term babies of smokers are born with narrowed airways and impaired lung function. Research released in 1994 found the children of mothers who smoked a half-pack of cigarettes [a day] or more during pregnancy had lower IQ scores than children whose mothers had not smoked. Studies also have shown that smoking in pregnancy can lead to delayed physical growth in children.

Clearly, pregnant women who quit smoking can contribute greatly to their child's health and well-being. However, recent findings reveal that quitting smoking may not be enough. Mothers need to protect their unborn children from other people's secondhand smoke as well. A 1995 study of 3,500 pregnant women found that nonsmoking women who were exposed to secondhand smoke during pregnancy had lower-birthweight babies than nonexposed expectant mothers.

TOBACCO INDUSTRY DENIAL

Americans most certainly should be worried about the toxic effects of secondhand smoke. What should worry them even more are the proponents of the tobacco industry who continue to deny not only the lethal effects of secondhand smoke but of smoking itself. For years, the tobacco industry has denied the health effects of smoking and secondhand smoke with accusations of poor science, questions about statistical significance and assertions of ignorance.

Perhaps Joseph A. Califano, then secretary of Health, Education and Welfare, responded most aptly to such tactics in his preface to the 1979 *Surgeon General's Report on Smoking and Health*:

> In truth, the attack upon the scientific and medical evidence about smoking is little more than an attack upon the science itself: an attack upon the epidemiological, clinical and experimental research disciplines upon which these conclusions are based. Like every attack upon science by vested interests, from Aristotle's day to Galileo's to our own, these attacks collapse of their own weight.

RESTRICTIONS ON PUBLIC SMOKING

In 1992, a Gallup survey conducted for the Coalition on Smoking or Health, cofounded by the American Lung Association, found that nine in 10 adults were aware that secondhand smoke is harmful to infants and young children, pregnant women and older healthy adults. Women were more likely than men to believe that secondhand smoke is harmful to all of these groups. Nonsmokers also were more likely than smokers strongly to agree about the harmful effects of secondhand smoke. An important finding was that even eight in 10 smokers know that secondhand smoke is bad for the people around them. The good news is that an increased percentage of those surveyed supported total bans or restrictions on smoking in public places such as restaurants, workplaces, hotels, buses and trains.

Forty-eight states and the District of Columbia have some restriction on smoking in public places. These laws range from designating a separate smoking area in schools to complete bans or restrictions on smoking in areas open to the public, including elevators, public buildings, restaurants, health facilities, public transportation, museums, shopping malls, retail stores and educational facilities. Among the states that limit or ban smoking in public areas, 43 restrict smoking in government workplaces and 23 restrict smoking in private-sector workplaces.

Since early 1990, smoking has been banned from almost all U.S. domestic airline flights. Most of today's travelers can barely remember the days of hazy, smoke-choked air travel. In recent years, many airlines have made some or all of their international flights smoke-free as well.

MORE NEEDS TO BE DONE

While progress certainly has been made toward reducing exposure to secondhand smoke, a great deal still needs to be accomplished. Thousands of corporate and restaurant employees throughout the country are exposed to harmful levels of secondhand smoke on a daily basis. In addition, a dangerous new trend in the form of "glamorous" cigar bars is exposing many to the harmful effects of secondhand cigar smoke.

Clearly, all Americans need to recognize and protect themselves and their children from the harmful effects of secondhand smoke. They should encourage the smokers in their lives to quit, and they should encourage their legislators to maintain or strengthen bans on smoking in public places. Only then can we breathe easy, knowing that our lungs and our lives aren't at risk from someone else's smoke.

> *"A major U.S. study ... failed to find a significant link between [secondhand smoke] and lung cancer."*

THE HARMFUL EFFECTS OF SECONDHAND SMOKE ARE EXAGGERATED

Jacob Sullum

In 1993, the Environmental Protection Agency (EPA) defined secondhand smoke as a cancer-causing agent, a contention that Jacob Sullum disputes in the following viewpoint. According to Sullum, the EPA's conclusions on secondhand smoke are based on faulty studies and mishandled statistics. In actuality, he contends, no substantial evidence links secondhand smoke to cancer. Furthermore, Sullum argues, the EPA's declaration about the alleged dangers of secondhand smoke is motivated by the current antismoking sentiment among policymakers and public health officials. Sullum is the senior editor of *Reason*, a monthly libertarian magazine.

As you read, consider the following questions:

1. In Sullum's opinion, why is exposure to secondhand smoke not analogous to cigarette smoking?
2. The EPA's conclusion about secondhand smoke was based on what kind of research, according to the author?
3. What is the conventional definition of a statistically significant result, according to Sullum?

"Secondhand Smoke Kills." So says a billboard on Pico Boulevard in Los Angeles that I pass every day on the way to work. I'm still not convinced. But most Americans seem to be: a CNN/*Time* poll conducted in March 1994 found that 78 per cent believe secondhand smoke is "very" or "somewhat" harmful.

That idea was endorsed by the U.S. Environmental Protection Agency (EPA) in 1993, when it declared secondhand smoke "a known human lung carcinogen." Since then the EPA's report has helped justify smoking bans throughout the country: in cities such as Los Angeles and San Francisco (likely to be joined soon by New York); in Maryland, Vermont, and Washington State; and in government offices, including the Defense Department. On March 25, 1994, the Occupational Safety and Health Administration proposed a ban on smoking in workplaces, including bars and restaurants. A bill introduced by Representative Henry Waxman (D., Calif.) would go even further, banning smoking in almost every building except residences. [Waxman's legislation did not pass.]

Most supporters of such measures probably believe that the EPA's report presents definitive scientific evidence that "secondhand smoke kills." But a closer look shows that the EPA manipulated data and finessed important points to arrive at a predetermined conclusion. The agency compromised science to support the political crusade against smoking.

A DECEPTIVE ANALOGY

The first line of defense for people who want to avoid scrutiny of the case against secondhand smoke (a/k/a environmental tobacco smoke, or ETS) is to argue by analogy. "We know that tobacco smoke causes disease and can kill you," says Scott Ballin, chairman of the Coalition on Smoking or Health. "It makes sense that a person who doesn't smoke cigarettes, who's sitting next to a smoker and inhaling the smoke, is also at some risk." The EPA offers a similar argument, devoting a chapter of its report on ETS to the evidence that smoking causes cancer.

Although superficially plausible, this analogy is misleading. A smoker breathes in hot, concentrated tobacco smoke and holds it in his lungs before exhaling. A nonsmoker in the vicinity, by contrast, breathes air that includes minute quantities of residual chemicals from tobacco smoke. "ETS is so highly diluted that it is not even appropriate to call it smoke," says Gary Huber, a professor of medicine at the University of Texas Health Science Center, writing with two colleagues in the July 1991 *Consumers' Research*. Furthermore, since many of the compounds in tobacco smoke are unstable, it is not safe to assume even that a non-smoker is exposed to the same chemicals as a smoker. Of 50 biologically active substances thought to be present in ETS, Huber and his colleagues report, only 14 have actually been detected.

Even if exposure to ETS were analogous to smoking, the doses involved are so small that it's not clear they would have any effect. Many chemicals that are hazardous or even fatal above a certain level are harmless (or beneficial) in smaller doses. James Enstrom, a professor of epidemiology at UCLA, estimates that someone exposed to ETS would be taking in the equivalent of a few cigarettes a year, perhaps one-hundredth of a cigarette a day. Yet studies of smoking have never looked at people who smoke that little; the lowest-exposure groups have been subjects who smoke up to five cigarettes a day.

FAULTY STUDIES

So it's not reasonable to conclude that ETS must be dangerous because smoking is dangerous. You have to look at the research that deals specifically with ETS. The EPA's finding is based on 30 epidemiological studies that compared lung-cancer rates among nonsmokers (mainly women) who lived with smokers to lung-cancer rates among nonsmokers who lived with nonsmokers. None of the studies measured actual exposure to ETS; they simply assumed that people who lived with smokers were more exposed than people who didn't. In most of these studies, lung cancer was somewhat more common among the subjects living with smokers, but in only 6 cases were the results statistically significant.

This is a crucial point. In any study that compares a group exposed to a suspected risk factor with a control group, the luck of the draw may result in a difference between the two groups that does not reflect a difference between the populations the groups are supposed to represent. Researchers do statistical tests to account for the possibility of such a fluke. By convention, epidemiologists call a result significant when the probability that it occurred purely by chance is 5 per cent or less. By this standard, 80 per cent of the studies discussed by the EPA did not find a statistically significant link between ETS and lung cancer.

But the EPA, which had always used the conventional definition of statistical significance in its risk assessments, adopted a different standard for the report on ETS. It considered a result significant if the probability that it occurred purely by chance was 10 per cent or less. This change essentially doubles the odds of being wrong. "The justification for this usage," according to the report itself, "is based on the *a priori* hypothesis . . . that a positive association exists between exposure to ETS and lung cancer." Of course, the EPA was supposed to *test* that hypothesis, not simply assume that it is true.

Instead of presenting results from the epidemiological studies as they originally appeared, the EPA recalculated them using the less rigorous standard. As a report from the Congressional Research Service drily notes, "it is unusual to return to a study after the fact, lower the required significance level, and declare its results to be supportive rather than unsupportive of the effect one's theory suggests should be present."

Even after the EPA massaged the data, the vast majority of the studies still did not show a significant association between ETS and lung cancer. Of the 11 U.S. studies, only 1 yielded a result that was significant according to the looser definition. (According to the usual definition, none of them did.) To bolster the evidence, the EPA did a "meta-analysis" of these studies. Dr. Enstrom notes that this technique was originally intended for clinical trials that assess the impact of a drug or procedure by randomly assigning subjects to treatment and control groups. By contrast, the data analyzed by the EPA came from retrospective case-control studies that "matched" people with lung cancer to people without lung cancer. Enstrom says using meta-analysis for such studies "is not a particularly meaningful exercise," because the studies are apt to differ in the way they define exposure, the confounding variables they take into account, the types of cancer they include, and so on.

In any event, the EPA's conclusion—that living with a smoker raises a woman's risk of getting lung cancer by 19 per cent—is justified only according to the definition of statistical significance adopted especially for these data. By the usual standard, even the meta-analysis does not support the claim that ETS causes lung cancer. Furthermore, the EPA excluded from its analysis a major U.S. study, published in the November 1992 *American Journal of Public Health*, that failed to find a significant link between ETS and lung cancer. Given the large size of the study, it could well have changed the outcome of the meta-analysis, so that the result would not have been significant even by the EPA's revised standard.

MISLEADING STATISTICS

Despite this "fancy statistical footwork," as a July 1992 article in *Science* described it, the EPA was able to claim only a weak association between ETS and lung cancer. With a risk increase as low as 19 per cent, it is difficult to rule out the possibility that other factors were at work. "At least 20 confounding variables have been identified as important to the development of lung cancer," write Huber et al. "No reported study comes anywhere close to controlling, or even mentioning, half of these."

Smokers tend to differ from nonsmokers in many ways—including diet, socioeconomic status, risk-taking behavior, and exercise—and it is likely that the spouses of smokers share these characteristics to some extent. "If wives of smokers share in poor health habits or other factors that could contribute to illness," the Congressional Research Service notes, "statistical associations found between disease and passive smoking could be incidental or misleading."

Misclassification could also account for some or all of the observed differences between wives of smokers and wives of nonsmokers. It's possible that some of the subjects thought to be nonsmokers were actually smokers or former smokers. Since spouses of smokers are more likely to be smokers themselves, such errors would have biased the results. The EPA adjusted the data to account for this effect, but it's impossible to say whether it fully compensated for misclassification.

These issues are especially important when the relationship between a suspected risk factor and a disease is weak. Based on the 11 U.S. studies, the EPA concluded that a woman who lives with a smoker is 1.19 times as likely to get lung cancer as a woman who lives with a nonsmoker. This ratio did not rise above 2.1 to 1 in any of the U.S. studies. In previous risk assessments, the EPA has seen such weak associations as cause for skepticism. When the agency examined the alleged connection between electromagnetic fields and cancer, for example, it said, "the association is not strong enough to constitute a proven causal relationship, largely because the relative risks in the published reports have seldom exceeded 3.0."

This concern did not prevent the EPA from reaching a firm conclusion about ETS, even though the agency recognized the limitations of the data. The head of the Scientific Advisory Board that reviewed the report conceded: "This is a classic case where the evidence is not all that strong."

The evidence is especially unimpressive when compared to the evidence that smoking causes lung cancer. In the latter case, there are thousands of studies, and virtually all of them have found a positive association, statistically significant in the vast majority of cases. And the associations are sizable: a typical female smoker is about 10 times as likely to get lung cancer as a female nonsmoker; for men the ratio is more like 20 to 1; and among heavy smokers, the figures are even higher. "The data on active smoking are so much stronger," Enstrom says. "That should be the focus of attention, not something which is so small and has the potential to be confounded by so many different things. I personally am baffled as to why people give it so much credibility."

UNIMPRESSIVE EVIDENCE

Publicity about a recent study on environmental tobacco smoke (ETS) and acute or chronic respiratory illnesses in children admonishes, "Children exposed to tobacco smoke . . . suffer over 10 million days of restricted activities . . . 21 percent more than unexposed kids." Ten million is a catchy, scary number, but where does it come from? The study appeared in the May 13–18, 1996, issue of the "scientific" journal, *Tobacco Control*, the very title of which should raise questions about scientific objectivity. The authors show right up front that they failed to find a "statistically significant" relationship between the children's exposure to tobacco smoke and any respiratory illnesses.

But then they reported that the parents in their sample were asked how many days the children missed school or had their activities restricted. Somehow, the researchers "found" here the relationship they wanted—albeit small. No attempt was made to determine if other factors could account for this, nor was there any attempt to account for the contradiction.

Sara Mahler-Vossler, *Insight*, June 16, 1997.

The explanation may be that the EPA's conclusion about ETS is useful in a way that the evidence about smoking is not. Although the share of adults who smoke has dropped from about 40 per cent to about 25 per cent since 1965, some 50 million Americans continue to smoke. And as Duke University economist W. Kip Viscusi shows in his book *Smoking: Making the Risky Decision*, this is not because they are ignorant about the health effects. Rather, they are willing to accept the risks in exchange for the benefits of smoking. From a "public-health" perspective, this is intolerable; no one should be allowed to make such a foolish decision. But the idea of protecting people from themselves still arouses considerable opposition in this country. Hence anti-smoking activists and public-health officials need a different excuse for restricting smoking: it endangers innocent bystanders.

When EPA Administrator Carol Browner testified in favor of Waxman's Smoke-Free Environment Act in February 1994, she relied heavily on the ETS report. But the main benefit that she claimed for the bill was its expected impact on smokers. "The reduction in smoker mortality due to smokers who quit, cut back, or do not start is estimated to range from about 33,000 to 99,000 lives per year," she said. And six surgeons general, reported the *New York Times*, "echoed the theme that this simple measure could do more for the public health than any other bill in years."

SHADING THE TRUTH

If your main goal is improving "the public health," you may be inclined to shade the truth a bit if it helps to make smoking less acceptable and more inconvenient. Marc Lalonde, Canada's former minister of national health and welfare, offered a rationale for such a strategy in a highly influential 1974 report: "Science is full of 'ifs,' 'buts,' and 'maybes,' while messages designed to influence the public must be loud, clear, and unequivocal. . . . The scientific 'yes, but' is essential to research, but for modifying human behavior of the population it sometimes produces the 'uncertain sound.' This is all the excuse needed by many to cultivate and tolerate an environment and lifestyle that is hazardous to health."

Writing about the ETS controversy in *Toxicologic Pathology*, Yale University epidemiologist Alvan Feinstein quotes a colleague who appears to have been influenced by the Lalonde Doctrine: "Yes, it's rotten science, but it's in a worthy cause. It will help us get rid of cigarettes and become a smoke-free society."

This seems to be the attitude that the EPA brought to its risk assessment. In June 1990 the agency released the first draft of *Environmental Tobacco Smoke: A Guide to Workplace Smoking Policies*, intended to advise employers to institute smoking restrictions. Yet this was three and a half years before the EPA officially determined that ETS was a health hazard. In a letter to Representative Thomas J. Bliley Jr. (R., Va.), then EPA Administrator William Reilly admitted that "beginning the development of an Agency risk assessment after the commencement of work on the draft policy guide gave the appearance of the very situation—i.e., policy leading science—that I am committed to avoid."

Reilly was so committed to avoiding this appearance that he decided not to release the final version of the policy guide, even though it was ready by December 1992. As he explained to the *Wall Street Journal*, putting out the guide along with the risk assessment would "look like we're trying to torque the science." But don't worry. Miss Browner, Mr. Reilly's successor, released the handy pamphlet in July 1993.

I"There is no safe use of tobacco."

SMOKELESS TOBACCO IS HARMFUL

Office of the Surgeon General

In the following viewpoint, the Office of the Surgeon General maintains that the use of smokeless tobacco can lead to oral cancer, cardiovascular disease, and nicotine addiction. Moreover, the authors point out, marketing strategies have made smokeless tobacco products attractive to first-time users and have created the erroneous perception that smokeless tobacco is harmless. This perception has increased the addictive potential of smokeless tobacco among younger users, who often "graduate" to using tobacco products with higher levels of nicotine, contends the Office of the Surgeon General. Furthermore, they argue, young people who use smokeless tobacco are more likely than non-users to smoke cigarettes, drink alcohol, and take drugs. The Office of the Surgeon General is part of the U.S. Department of Health and Human Services.

As you read, consider the following questions:
1. According to the authors, what percentage of high school males report recent use of smokeless tobacco?
2. What is leukoplakia, according to the authors?
3. According to the Office of the Surgeon General, what percentage of smokeless tobacco users also smoke cigarettes?

Reprinted from "Youth and Tobacco: Preventing Tobacco Use Among Young People," a report from the Office of the Surgeon General, Department of Health and Human Services, Washington, D.C., 1994.

S mokeless tobacco includes two main types: chewing tobacco and snuff. These products are made from the same type of dark- or burley-leaved tobacco. Most smokeless tobacco is grown in Kentucky, Pennsylvania, Tennessee, Virginia, West Virginia, and Wisconsin. Leaves are generally aged one to three years, but snuff tobacco leaves are aged longer than chewing tobacco leaves. People who use chewing tobacco place a wad of loose-leaf tobacco or a plug of compressed tobacco in their cheek; snuff users place a small amount of powdered or finely cut tobacco (loose or wrapped in a paper pouch) between their gum and cheek. Smokeless tobacco users then suck on the tobacco and spit out the tobacco juices with accompanying saliva. As a consequence of the way in which smokeless products are used, smokeless tobacco is sometimes referred to as spit or spitting tobacco.

THE DANGERS OF SMOKELESS TOBACCO

The most notable health consequences associated with smokeless tobacco use include halitosis (bad breath), discoloration of teeth and fillings, abrasion of teeth, dental caries, gum recession, leukoplakia, nicotine dependence, and various forms of oral cancer. Specifically, smokeless tobacco use has been implicated in cancers of the gum, mouth, pharynx, larynx, and esophagus and has also been indicated in early reports of the development of verrucous carcinoma. Smokeless tobacco use may also play a role in cardiovascular disease and stroke, through increases in blood pressure, vasoconstriction, and irregular heartbeat. Since nearly 25 percent of adult smokeless tobacco users also smoke cigarettes, the effects on the oral cavity may be synergistic, and the risks of developing cancer of the oral cavity and pharynx noticeably increase.

WHO USES SMOKELESS TOBACCO?

The 1986 Surgeon General's report on smokeless tobacco use concluded that there is no safe use of tobacco. Despite that report and subsequent legislation, restrictions, and follow-up reports, smokeless tobacco use in the United States remains a serious concern. The use of smokeless tobacco by adults has remained relatively constant at about 5 percent for males and 1 percent for females. However, smokeless tobacco use among high school males has become markedly more prevalent in the past two decades; about 20 percent report using smokeless tobacco recently. In some states, nearly one out of three high school males uses smokeless tobacco. There is little indication that use among young people is significantly declining.

Smokeless tobacco use primarily begins in early adolescence; some research indicates an average age of onset of 10 years. Among high school seniors who had regularly used smokeless tobacco, 23 percent reported that they had first tried the product by the sixth grade, and 53 percent by the eighth grade.

HEALTH CONSEQUENCES

A 1992 report of the Office of Inspector General concluded that smokeless tobacco use causes serious, but generally not fatal, short-term health consequences among young people. The primary health consequences during adolescence include leukoplakia, gum recession, nicotine addiction, and increased risk of becoming a cigarette smoker. Leukoplakia and/or gum recession occur in 40 to 60 percent of smokeless tobacco users.

Leukoplakia has been defined by the World Health Organization as a lesion of the soft tissue that consists of a white patch (mucosal macule) or plaque that cannot be scraped off. R.O. Greer and T.C. Poulson (1983) examined 117 high school students who were smokeless tobacco users; oral soft-tissue lesions were found in 49 percent of these students. Oral leukoplakias carry a five-year malignant transformation potential of about 5 percent. If smokeless tobacco use ceases, the leukoplakia appears to regress or resolve entirely.

Gingival tissue recession (or gum recession) commonly occurs in the area of the oral cavity immediately adjacent to where smokeless tobacco is held. When smokeless tobacco remains exclusively in a specific intraoral location, gingival recession occurs among 30 percent to over 90 percent of users. T. Modéer, S. Lavstedt, and C. Åhlund (1980) found that snuff use among 13- and 14-year-old students could directly affect the gingival tissues, causing gingivitis, or gum inflammation. In a study of 565 adolescent male students with gingivitis in Georgia, S. Offenbacher and D.R. Weathers (1985) found that gingival recession was significantly more prevalent, and the odds of developing this condition were nine times greater, among smokeless tobacco users than among nonusers. Navy recruits from 45 states were examined to determine if smokeless tobacco use was associated with gingival recession. Results of the study showed that 31 percent of heavy users and 19 percent of nonusers or low users had gingival recession. Users' age and the intensity of smokeless tobacco use were significant factors in explaining variations in the degree of gingival recession. Two additional studies of adolescents failed to show an association between the use of smokeless tobacco and gingival recession, possibly because most of the users had been using the product for a short time.

NICOTINE ADDICTION

The addictive qualities of smokeless tobacco are also a matter of major concern. Smokeless tobacco users develop a nicotine dependency similar to that of cigarette smokers. This is not surprising, since smokeless tobacco users absorb at least as much nicotine as smokers do—perhaps as much as twice the amount. The high pH of saliva favors absorption of nicotine through oral mucosa, and the degree of absorption increases with the increasing pH of the tobacco product. The rate of absorption of nicotine from snuff is particularly rapid. With continued use of smokeless tobacco, blood nicotine levels remain relatively high; these levels fall more slowly after smokeless tobacco is removed from the mouth than after a cigarette has been smoked.

SMOKELESS TOBACCO CAUSES CANCER

Smokeless tobacco products, which include snuff and chewing tobacco, cause cancer in humans. Smokeless tobacco contains at least 28 known carcinogens, including nitrosamines, benzo[a]-pyrene, formaldehyde and polonium-210. Users of smokeless tobacco are at least four to six times more likely than nonusers to develop cancer of the oral cavity or pharynx and are up to 50 times more likely to develop cancer of the gums and the lining of the cheeks. Several studies suggest that smokeless tobacco users may also be at increased risk for other cancers. The high prevalence of smokeless tobacco use among African-American men in past decades probably accounts for a considerable portion of their death rate from oral and pharyngeal cancers, a rate that since 1980 has been more than double the rate for white men. Further, we may soon see an increase in overall oral and pharyngeal cancer rates due to the explosion in the popularity of smokeless tobacco that began a decade or so ago among young white men.

Scott L. Tomar, Priorities, vol. 7, no. 4, 1995.

Adolescents develop physical dependence from smokeless tobacco use, as is evidenced by their experience of withdrawal symptoms when they try to quit. Smokeless tobacco cessation produces withdrawal symptoms that are similar to those for smoking cessation, including cravings, irritability, distractibility, and hunger. Adolescents who are most addicted to nicotine appear to be less able to quit. Thus, as is seen with cigarette use, adolescents who are heavy smokeless tobacco users are likely to become adult users.

The addictive potential of smokeless tobacco use is aggravated by the fact that some smokeless products are highly effective in the initiation process and are even termed "starter products" by one smokeless tobacco company. These products tend to be low in nicotine concentration and low in pH (thus reducing absorption); some are in a unit dosage form ("tobacco pouch"), which helps first-time users avoid placing too much of the substance in their mouths. These products may have contributed to the reversal of the demographics of smokeless tobacco users from 1970 to 1986. In 1970, the majority of smokeless tobacco users were 50 years old and older; by 1986, the majority were 35 years old and younger. Marketing and advertising factors have been identified as having instilled the general perception that smokeless tobacco products are safe and socially acceptable. Marketing strategies included a heavy reliance on distributing free samples of product types designed to introduce new users to what one company termed the "graduation process." Advertising strategies then encouraged new users to experience greater "satisfaction" and "pleasure" by switching to maintenance products higher in nicotine concentration and pH.

A Risk Factor for Smoking and Drug Use

Young people who use smokeless tobacco appear to be at greater risk to smoke cigarettes than are nonusers. Among smokeless tobacco users, 12 to 43 percent also smoke cigarettes. In a 1986–1989 study, 44 percent of high school seniors had tried both smokeless tobacco and cigarettes; of those, 63 percent had tried smokeless tobacco either before or at about the same time as cigarettes. In a prospective study, D.V. Ary, E. Lichtenstein, and H.H. Severson (1987) found that smokeless tobacco users were significantly more likely than nonusers to initiate cigarette smoking. Smokeless tobacco users were also more likely to increase their use of cigarettes over a one-year period. For adolescents who use both smokeless tobacco and cigarettes, cessation of one substance may lead to a direct increase in the other.

Smokeless tobacco use is also predictive of other drug use. In a study of more than 3,000 male adolescents interviewed twice at nine-month intervals about their use of various psychoactive substances, the main findings were that (1) smokeless tobacco users were significantly more likely to use cigarettes, marijuana, or alcohol than nonusers, (2) users of smokeless tobacco were significantly more likely to take up the use of these other substances by the second interview if they were not using them at the first, and (3) adolescents who were using any of these substances at the first interview were significantly more likely to increase their use of the substance if they also used smokeless tobacco.

Two other facts are important to consider when evaluating the role of smokeless tobacco products in the use of cigarettes and other substances. First, the overall impact of smokeless tobacco is currently limited primarily to males (the main users of these substances). Second, smokeless tobacco users in the Ary, Lichtenstein, and Severson (1987) study, as well as in most other surveys, tend to initiate their tobacco use at about the same age as cigarette smokers or at a slightly earlier age.

I"Smokeless tobacco is a lifesaver."

SMOKELESS TOBACCO CAN BENEFIT PUBLIC HEALTH

Brad Rodu and Philip Cole

In the following viewpoint, Brad Rodu and Philip Cole argue that the use of smokeless tobacco is not as harmful as cigarette smoking and could actually help people who need nicotine while trying to quit smoking. According to the authors, smokeless tobacco does not cause respiratory illness, lung cancer, or heart disease; nor does it expose nonsmokers to the dangers of secondhand smoke. Smokers who switch to smokeless tobacco decrease their own health risks while benefiting public health, they contend. Rodu is a professor of oral pathology at the University of Alabama in Birmingham and author of *For Smokers Only: How Smokeless Tobacco Can Save Your Life*. Cole is a professor of epidemiology at the University of Alabama in Birmingham.

As you read, consider the following questions:
1. What is the only significant health risk for users of smokeless tobacco, according to Rodu and Cole?
2. How does the life expectancy of a user of smokeless tobacco compare with the life expectancy of a smoker, according to the authors?
3. Why are newer smokeless tobacco products preferable to old-fashioned chewing tobacco, in the authors' opinion?

From "Would a Switch from Cigarettes to Smokeless Tobacco Benefit Public Health: Yes," by Brad Rodu and Philip Cole, *Priorities*, vol. 7, no. 4, 1995. Reprinted with permission from *Priorities*, a publication of the American Council on Science and Health, 1995 Broadway, 2nd Floor, New York, NY 10023-5860.

S mokeless Tobacco Is A Lifesaver. This message of hope for millions of smokers is based on three facts. First, smokeless tobacco use is 98 percent safer than cigarette smoking. Thus, it can save the lives of smokers and of those persons who breathe secondhand smoke. Second, smokeless tobacco effectively provides the nicotine kick smokers crave. That is why one third of smokeless users in the U.S. today are former smokers, according to the Centers for Disease Control and Prevention (CDC). Third—and this may be surprising to most readers—modern smokeless tobacco products can be used invisibly, much like a breath mint, in any social situation. This is important because old-fashioned "chewing" or "spitting" tobacco is outdated and irrelevant to this discussion. These facts are the foundation of a simple and practical harm reduction strategy for inveterate smokers: switch to smokeless tobacco.

This "switch-to-smokeless" strategy has major implications for public health efforts regarding tobacco use, and thus several issues arise. Does the proposal have a sound scientific rationale? Is it practical enough for widespread implementation? Will smokers who switch to smokeless tobacco remain addicted to nicotine, instead of quitting altogether? Is it appropriate to recommend a preventive strategy that carries some risk? Will nonusers of tobacco, especially teenagers, infer that smokeless tobacco use is safe? Discussion of these issues will provide a new framework for the examination of cigarette smoking, America's single most avoidable cause of death.

THE SCIENTIFIC RATIONALE

According to the CDC 46 million Americans smoke, and 419,000 of them die annually from smoking-related illnesses such as heart and circulatory diseases, lung cancer and emphysema. The price smokers pay in terms of reduced life expectancy is staggering. We reported in a 1994 paper published in *Nature* that lifelong smokers live an average of eight years less than do nonusers of tobacco.

Contrary to a popular misperception, all forms of tobacco are not equally risky. Smokeless tobacco causes neither lung cancer nor other diseases of the lung, and users have no excess risk for heart attacks. In fact, the only consequential—but infrequent—adverse health effect of smokeless tobacco use is oral cancer. In 1981, writing in the *New England Journal of Medicine*, Dr. Deborah Winn and colleagues established that smokeless tobacco users are four times more likely to develop oral cancer than are nonusers of tobacco. However, this relative risk is only about one half the relative risk of oral cancer from smoking.

In Table 1 we compare directly the annual mortality of 46 million smokers with an equal number of smokeless tobacco users. The number of deaths from smoking is almost 70 times higher than the number from smokeless tobacco use. In terms of life expectancy, the smokeless tobacco user loses only about 15 days on average, compared with the eight years lost by the smoker.

TABLE 1: ANNUAL TOBACCO-RELATED MORTALITY IN 46 MILLION—SMOKERS VS. SMOKELESS TOBACCO USERS

	Smokers	Smokeless Tobacco Users
From cancer	151,000	6,000
(mouth cancer)	(11,500)	(6,000)
From heart and circulatory disease	180,000	0
From respiratory disease	85,000	0
Miscellaneous	3,000	0
	419,000	6,000
Years of Life Lost (Average)	7.8	0.04

Adapted from: 1. Centers for Disease Control, *Morbidity and Mortality Weekly* Report 42, 1993. 2. Brad Rodu, *American Journal of the Medical Sciences* 308, 1994. 3. Brad Rodu and Philip Cole, *Nature* 370, 1994.

Another major health benefit: smokers who switch to smokeless tobacco produce no passive smoke to harm others. The American Heart Association estimates that 40,000 Americans die annually from diseases related to secondhand smoke. No one dies from the secondary effects of smokeless tobacco use. Thus, this proposal could be recommended solely on the basis of lives saved through the elimination of the effects of passive smoking.

These published facts are, insofar as we are aware, unrefuted. But a transition to smokeless tobacco is not merely a scientifically based strategy of smoking cessation; it is already a practical reality.

FROM SCIENCE TO PRACTICE

Statistics from the CDC indicate that more than 1.5 million smokers have used smokeless tobacco to quit smoking. The transition is possible because the spike of nicotine that addicted smokers seek is effectively delivered by smokeless tobacco. Furthermore, newer smokeless tobacco products are essentially invisible in use, as they occupy no more space than a breath mint

or a piece of chewing gum. A small, pre-packaged pouch of tobacco is tucked discreetly between the cheek and gum, where it
delivers nicotine across the lining of the mouth. Spitting, once
the stigma of outmoded and bulky "chewing" tobacco, is minimal or nonexistent. We recently published the first profiles of a
group of "switchers." They came from all walks of life and
switched to smokeless tobacco after smoking many years (25
years on average). Some switched to smokeless after months or
years of abstinence and continuous craving. The transition
proved stable in this group, as the average duration of smokeless
tobacco use after quitting smoking was nine years.

What do switchers accomplish? Our research shows that they
will live, on average, as long as those smokers who quit nicotine
altogether. They reduce their risks for smoking-related illness and
death, which is the goal of all existing smoking cessation efforts.
There is, of course, no debate about the ideal way to achieve this
goal: complete tobacco abstinence. But that ideal is not always at-
tainable since many smokers are unable to give up nicotine.
Switching to smokeless tobacco is a small compromise with the
ideal that reaps large individual and public health gains.

Judging Nicotine

Smokeless tobacco provides the former smoker with nicotine.
This seems to pose a problem only to staunch anti-tobacco activists who are committed to total tobacco abstinence. It is true
that some persons who switch might otherwise quit tobacco
entirely. But there are millions of smokers who cannot quit, for
existing quit-smoking methods are minimally successful. Let's
face reality: Each year 419,000 nicotine addicts do not quit
soon enough to avoid a premature death. Why compel nicotine-
seeking smokers to choose only between inhaling tobacco
smoke and abstinence? Smokers who switch to smokeless tobacco can still strive for nicotine abstinence after the delivery
system has been changed.

We emphasize that nicotine is the reason people smoke but
not the reason that smokers die. In the fall of 1995 a Food and
Drug Administration (FDA) advisory panel echoed our sentiment when it recommended that nicotine gum be released from
prescription status in order to make it more widely available.
With this action the panel supports our position: that quitting
smoking—without necessarily quitting nicotine—is the key to
reducing health risks. Smokeless tobacco, which is already available without prescription, is another acceptable alternative.

Health professionals often recommend prevention strategies

that carry small risks. For example, the National Cancer Institute (NCI) is evaluating the drug tamoxifen as a preventive agent for women with a high risk for breast cancer. However, although tamoxifen may reduce breast cancer risk, it increases the risk of cancer of the uterus. The NCI believes that the benefits from tamoxifen may outweigh the risks. Substituting smokeless tobacco for smoking is a wise risk-reduction strategy because it reduces *all* smoking-related risks and introduces *no* new risks.

It has been suggested that it is not appropriate for health professionals to recommend smokeless tobacco for smokers because the patient-switcher might develop mouth cancer. But concerned physicians and dentists understand that it is their moral and ethical obligation to help patients make informed lifestyle choices, all of which involve benefits and risks. One example is the recommendation to substitute oral methadone for intravenous heroin, a practice approved by the FDA in 1973 and now an accepted harm-reduction alternative for heroin users. Providing information about an alternative to smoking that is 98 percent safer is not only consistent with the highest standards of medical ethics, it is mandated by them.

For Smokers Only

Will nonusers of tobacco, especially teenagers, misinterpret our message and begin smokeless tobacco use? It is possible, so we have directed our message carefully and specifically to adult smokers. We are opposed to tobacco initiation by anyone. But we recognize that tobacco initiation is a complicated matter, more influenced by peer pressure and parental usage than by a scientific discussion of tobacco risks. History tells us that in spite of society's best efforts, some portion of the population has always been addicted to tobacco. In its concern over tobacco initiation, society cannot deny adult smokers medical information permitting them to lead longer and healthier lives. Our message does not represent tobacco promotion, but tobacco pragmatism.

Rethinking Tobacco Control

The past 30 years have brought ever more assertive public health campaigns against cigarette smoking. A coalition of well-funded public and private agencies has as its goal a reduction in the prevalence of cigarette smoking. The coalition's influence has resulted in pervasive health warnings, ever more intensive quit-smoking programs, and recently the social ostracism of smokers and the industry that supplies them. Yet many Americans continue to smoke, and far too many die from smoking-related diseases.

In this viewpoint we have presented the scientific foundation and practical rationale for a thorough rethinking of tobacco control policies and their premises. Our proposal empowers smokers to gain control over the consequences of their nicotine addiction. It also empowers society to avoid burdensome and intrusive tobacco control measures—those involving unnecessary legislation, regulation and litigation—that have become popular recently. Since our proposal is entirely unintrusive and solely educational, it has a strong fundamental, moral rationale and so will be welcomed both by smokers and the health care professionals who take care of them.

Periodical Bibliography

The following articles have been selected to supplement the diverse views presented in this chapter. Addresses are provided for periodicals not indexed in the *Readers' Guide to Periodical Literature*, the *Alternative Press Index*, the *Social Sciences Index*, or the *Index to Legal Periodicals and Books*.

George Bain	"A Phoney Debate over Cigarette Addiction," *Maclean's*, August 26, 1996.
Carl E. Bartecchi, Thomas D. MacKenzie, and Robert W. Schrier	"The Human Costs of Tobacco Use," Part I, *New England Journal of Medicine*, March 31, 1994. Available from 10 Shattuck St., Boston, MA 02115-6094.
Joyce L. Bennett	"That Demon Weed," *Chronicles*, February 1997. Available from the Rockford Institute, 934 N. Main St., Rockford, IL 61103-7061.
Peter L. Berger	"Furtive Smokers—and What They Tell Us About America," *Commentary*, June 1994.
Congressional Digest	Special issue on congressional testimony about secondhand tobacco smoke, May 1994.
Kendall Hamilton	"Blowing Smoke," *Newsweek*, July 21, 1997.
Suein L. Hwang and Alix M. Freedman	"Smokers May Mistake 'Clean' Cigarette for Safe," *Wall Street Journal*, April 30, 1996.
JAMA	Special section on tobacco use, April 24, 1996. Available from Subscriber Services Center, American Medical Association, 515 N. State St., Chicago, IL 60610.
Ross Kerber	"Do Approved Cigarette Tests Understate Tar?" *Wall Street Journal*, January 30, 1997.
David Lamb	"Relishing the Joy of Smoking," *Los Angeles Times*, November 5, 1996. Available from Reprints, Times Mirror Square, Los Angeles, CA 90053.
Kai Maristen	"Nicotine, an Autobiography," *American Scholar*, Summer 1996.
Jacob Sullum	"Passive Reporting on Passive Smoke," *Forbes Media Critic*, Summer 1994.
Kenneth E. Warner et al.	"The Emerging Market for Long-Term Nicotine Maintenance," *JAMA*, October 1, 1997.

SHOULD TOBACCO ADVERTISING BE RESTRICTED?

Chapter Preface

Numerous studies have found that most smokers start smoking when they are in their teens. If they do not start smoking before age eighteen, chances are they will never start. Antismoking groups charge that tobacco companies know this fact well, and they combat it by targeting children in their advertising.

Antismoking groups contend that R.J. Reynolds (RJR) and other tobacco companies have deliberately targeted minors in their cigarette advertising. They cite secret memos written by cigarette companies during the 1970s and 1980s that outlined advertising strategies for attracting "younger smokers," defined in the memos as those between ages thirteen and twenty-four. Furthermore, they contend that these memos show that the popular cartoon figure Joe Camel was developed by RJR because "comic strip–type copy might get a much higher readership among younger people than any other type of copy." Using cartoon figures such as Joe Camel in advertising has definitely encouraged children to emulate the cool Joe Camel, the critics charge.

The tobacco industry, including R.J. Reynolds, insists, however, that it does not direct its advertising at minors. RJR maintains that the age listed in its memo is a typographical error and should have read eighteen, not thirteen. Furthermore, the company contends, the memos cited by the antismoking groups were "cherry-picked" and taken out of context. R.J. Reynolds's "position and policy have remained constant," the company maintains in a 1998 statement. "Smoking is a choice for adults," not for children. Tobacco companies also assert that peer pressure and family example, not advertising, are the primary reasons why teenagers start smoking.

After the Federal Trade Commission threatened to ban Joe Camel from cigarette ads in 1997, R.J. Reynolds agreed to drop the cartoon figure from its advertising. The controversy over the role advertising plays in encouraging minors to smoke is far from over, however, as can be seen from the material in the following chapter.

| "Advertising is the most potent force
in causing children to start smoking."

TOBACCO ADVERTISING ENCOURAGES TEENS TO SMOKE

William Everett Bailey

In the following viewpoint, William Everett Bailey argues that children are the only segment of the population who readily respond to advertising. Tobacco companies realize this, he contends, and target much of their advertising toward children. Furthermore, Bailey maintains, studies show that the number of teenage smokers increases in direct response to certain cigarette advertising campaigns. Bailey is the author of *The Invisible Drug*, from which this viewpoint is taken.

As you read, consider the following questions:

1. According to a study by the Centers for Disease Control and Prevention, which group of teenagers was reported to have the largest increase in the number of smokers, as cited by Bailey?
2. How do cigarette advertising strategies seduce children and teens into smoking, in the author's opinion?
3. What precipitated the sharpest increase in teen smoking, according to Bailey?

Tobacco advertising has one purpose—to get people to smoke. Advertising was the motivating factor to get masses of women to start smoking in the 1920's. Today, it just so happens that the only group that responds to tobacco ads are children. Advertising is the most potent force in causing children to start smoking. The alarming rise in teen smoking is also attributed to peer pressure, easy access to cigarettes, and the feeling of immortality.

THE ALARMING TRENDS IN CHILDREN SMOKING

During a six-year cigarette advertising blitz, from 1967 to 1973, there was a tremendous increase in young women starting to smoke. Doctors at the University of California, San Diego, (UCSD) Cancer Center observed this horrifying smoking trend among young girls:

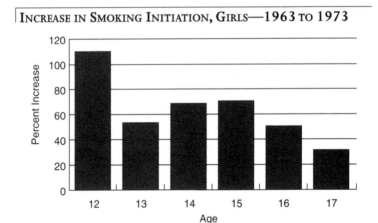

INCREASE IN SMOKING INITIATION, GIRLS—1963 TO 1973

William Everett Bailey, *The Invisible Drug*, 1996.

The researchers found twelve-year-old girls showed the biggest increase in smoking. On the other hand, they found no increase in boys starting to smoke during the same time. They concluded that advertising has an important impact on the uptake of smoking by girls, and does play a role in encouraging long-term nicotine addiction. Since that time, girls have started smoking at the same rate, and in some areas higher than boys. The UCSD doctors urged a ban on all advertising and promotion of cigarettes.

Teen smoking dropped from 1976 to 1984, then leveled off. The downhill slide in teen smoking was effectively stopped by a corresponding change in cigarette promotion budgets in 1991 which increased 16%. The following year, teen smoking again started increasing steadily.

In 1996, the Centers for Disease Control (CDC) reported that the percentage of high school teens reporting that they smoked within the last 30 days rose dramatically from 27.5% in 1991 to 34.8% in 1995. By race and sex, the single largest increase in smoking was among black male teens, which increased 14%. Even more alarming, 16% of all teens surveyed reported smoking at least 20 cigarettes per month. One pack a month is enough to induce nicotine cravings, and explains why 20% of high school graduates are addicted to nicotine.

Dr. J. DeFranza, author of a study published in the *Journal of the American Medical Association,* found that adolescents smoke 947 million packs of cigarettes and consume 26 million packages of smokeless tobacco a year. Children eight to 11 years old that smoked daily averaged four per day, and those 12 to 17 years smoked an average 14 a day. It takes millions of children smoking seven to 14 cigarettes a day to spend $1.26 billion on tobacco annually.

Consider these trends:

- Three million kids under 18 smoke.
- 3,000 teens a day, 1.1 million teens a year, start smoking.
- 19.4% of high school seniors smoked daily in 1994, up from 18.5% in 1991.
- Nine percent of eighth graders smoked daily in 1994, up from 7.2% in 1991.
- 75% of adolescent smokers want to quit, but cannot.
- 70% of adolescent smokers say they would not have started smoking if they could choose again.
- 14½ years is the average age when smoking begins.
- 90% of new smokers are under 19 years of age.
- 50% of new teen smokers will smoke at least 16 to 20 years.

ADVERTISING STARTS CHILDREN SMOKING

Decades ago, tobacco advertising attracted new adult smokers. When it no longer attracted new adult smokers, marketing strategies had to change. Tobacco companies had to replace the smokers that quit or died every year with new smokers. Tobacco advertising and promotion took an abrupt turn to address their potential loss of profit. They started targeting kids, and it worked—teens started smoking by the millions. Consider that 90% of smoking initiation starts before age 19. For all practical purposes tobacco advertising only works on teens 19 years old and younger. The National Center for Chronic Disease Prevention says that advertising is to blame for 3,000 teens a day starting to smoke. In contrast, there has been a decrease in the number of children smoking in countries like New Zealand, where tobacco advertising has been banned. In America today, some $1 billion in cigarettes are sold every year to three million teens.

Research shows that advertising does affect the uptake and the continuation of smoking by children. Doctors at the University of California, San Diego, reported in the *Journal of the National Cancer Institute,* that "tobacco marketing may be a stronger current influence in encouraging adolescents to initiate the smoking uptake process than exposure to peer or family smokers." Dr. John P. Pierce, an author of the study, says that "receptivity to tobacco advertising is twice as good an indicator of whether a child will smoke as whether peers or family members are smokers."

KIDS SMOKE THE MOST HEAVILY ADVERTISED BRANDS

A report on adolescent smoking by the CDC confirmed they smoke the most heavily advertised brands. Furthermore, adolescents changed brand preferences as brand-specific advertising increased.

A California survey in 1990 found that teens smoke the top two most heavily advertised brands: Marlboro and Camel. The authors concluded that cigarette advertisements do encourage teens to smoke. In the interest of public health, they suggested banning all tobacco advertisements.

A more recent national survey of teen smokers, age 12 to 18 years, found similar trends in cigarette brand selection. From 1989 to 1993, the most popular brand smoked was Marlboro; Camel was the second, and Newport was third. Most disturbing, 85% of adolescent smokers choose one of these three most heavily advertised brands. And at the heart of the problem, spending on regional cigarette advertising correlates with the brands adolescents smoke in that region. These observations establish a positive link of cigarette advertising to adolescents' brand preference. . . .

These three brands, Marlboro, Camel, and Newport, have a higher teen market share for each advertising dollar spent than other brands. The advertisements for the other brands studied, Kool, Merit, Salem, Virginia Slims, Winston and Benson & Hedges, were less appealing to kids and did not have the same effect on teen market share. [Professor Richard W.] Pollay commented on this data saying it "clearly shows that cigarette advertising for market share is primarily a battle of brands for consumption by the young.". . .

PREDATOR TARGETS THEIR PREY

Cigarette advertising strategies today seduce children and teens into smoking by associating it with a protest of authority figures, rebellion, and a symbol of independence. They present tobacco as desirable, socially acceptable, glamorous, something cool, safe and healthy. Smoking is also presented as more prevalent in society than it actually is. The ads are so convincing that smoking will bring happiness, that teenage girls suffering from depression and anxiety will smoke thinking it will relieve their psychiatric symptoms.

Cigarette ads create a desire—a desire to be popular, to be accepted. The ads remind the youngsters of what they lack, and imply that smoking will satisfy that lack. Men and women, real or cartoon characters, are depicted having fun, and doing adult things which teens want to do. Teens project themselves into the picture enjoying those things—taking risks, enjoying adult activities, being comfortable in social situations and smoking.

SELLING A COMMODITY TO STARTERS

The number one rule of selling is: know your customer. That is precisely why the tobacco industry sponsored research to learn how tobacco smoking starts. They identified the major psychological vulnerabilities of children, who they call starters. These psychological vulnerabilities are used to sell perceived social benefits, such as improved self-image and self-confidence, individuality, popularity, and admiration by peers. As one tobacco company memo put it, "At a younger age, taste requirements and satisfaction of a cigarette are thought to play a secondary role to the social requirements."

In 1973, RJR [R.J. Reynolds Tobacco Co.] proposed tailoring cigarette marketing to the 21 and under group. "Realistically, if our company is to survive and prosper, over the long term," wrote Claude Teague Jr., RJR assistant director of research and development, "we must get our share of the youth market." "This is clear and convincing evidence," explains Scott Ballin, of the Coalition on Smoking OR Health, "that they are targeting kids." RJR claims they never acted on the memo.

On July 3, 1974, D.W. Tredennick, a RJR marketing research executive, wrote about their advertising and how to attract new smokers: "young smokers wear their cigarette, and it becomes a part of the 'I' they wish to be." He went on to say that young smokers choose a cigarette brand because of "the user image a brand projects and differentiated product characteristics." Even more interesting, Tredennick noted that smoking "generally starts during the teens," and that half became regular smokers by the age of 18. Three years later in 1977, a RJR Marketing Plan positioned Salem to "Emulate personalities and situational elements that are compatible with the aspirations and lifestyles of contemporary young adults."

Tobacco company marketing executives must constantly think of new ways to attract potential candidates for nicotine use. A B.A.T. [British-American Tobacco] Viceroy brand market research plan in 1975 revealed a strategy to create a desire to smoke in starters. The Viceroy plan suggested: "For the young, smoking is not a part of day-to-day life, it is part of an illicit pleasure category." The plan suggested to relate smoking to something "bad," to portray it as part of growing-up.

"PRESENT SMOKING AS AN ILLICIT PLEASURE"

This image was created with ambiguous pictures, to reduce objections and to repress health concerns. Cigarettes were touted to help in tense social situations. B.A.T.'s advertising thrust used to attract starters to Viceroy was:

- Present smoking as an initiation into the adult world.
- Present smoking as an illicit pleasure category of product and activities.
- Symbolize growing-up, the maturity process.
- Avoid health concerns!

B.A.T. sued a Chicago CBS anchorman in 1981 for stating that B.A.T.'s marketing strategy was to link Viceroy's to illicit pleasures such as marijuana, and to sex.

PEER PRESSURE ADVERTISING

Peer pressure advertising can apply the same forces that a friend or family member can. Peer pressure advertising must attack at the vulnerable age of 11 to 12 years, when the desire to be part of a peer group is the strongest.

Tempo by RJR was a peer pressure brand. RJR's marketing strategy was to use positive imagery. An attractive social appearance and peer group acceptance were pitched in the ads—the psychological benefits the insecure child desires. More recently, RJR used Joe Camel peer pressure ads. The ads depict Joe rejecting a cowboy, a Marlboro type man. This switch advertising has a peer pressure twist and says if you smoke Marlboro you are not cool and you are not welcome.

RJR claims that they never acted on the memos from the 1970's that spoke of targeting teens with cigarette ads. Despite their denial, RJR embarked on a program called (YAS) Young Adult Smokers. YAS consisted of one element to address the fact that a smoker's first cigarette brand is the brand they are most likely to smoke for years. The YAS promotion was intended to target 18 to 24 year olds.

HIGH SCHOOL KIDS ARE SMOKING MORE

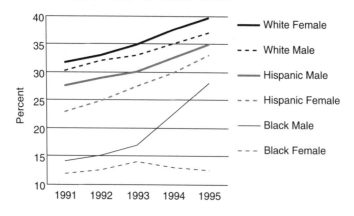

William Everett Bailey, *The Invisible Drug*, 1996.

Despite their alleged intentions, in 1990 RJR divisional managers targeted stores frequented by young shoppers for special YAS cigarette logo consumer items. Memos written by two RJR managers instructed their salespeople to target stores in this manner: "These stores can be in close proximity to colleges (and) high schools." "Identify these accounts . . . in the general vicinity of the high schools."

RJR's YAS program was very effective in capturing the youth market for Camel. Camel became the most popular brand of smokers under 18 years old. Following the first year of the YAS promotion, Camel market share of young smokers rose from 3% to 8.1 %. By 1991, it had risen to 13%. Richard J. Durbin, IL-D, Congressional Task Force on Tobacco, said "They are going after American kids with a vengeance."

If the industry actually used this sales strategy, more tobacco advertisements would be found in stores near schools. In 1995, the California Department of Health Services studied 5,700 stores in the state. They found an interesting correlation between the number of cigarette promotional items in stores and its proximity to high schools. Stores within 1,000 feet of a school had an average of 26.5 ads per store, and an average of 5.6 exterior ads. Those over 1,000 feet, averaged 24.9 ads per store, with only 4.5 ads on the outside. Stores in young neighborhoods, with one-third of the population 17 years and younger, had the highest number of ads per store.

Not only were there more ads at the stores closer to schools, and in young neighborhoods, something more shocking was discovered. The tobacco ads were near the candy counters, and placed only three feet above the floor. If these ads were intended for adults to see, they would be at eye level of an adult, but instead are at the eye level of a child. In 1993, tobacco companies spent $1.6 billion on cash slotting fees (a fee paid to the retailer for each carton or package "face" that is visible to the customer), and promotional items, such as caps and T-shirts, to enhance tobacco sales in retail stores.

It should not be difficult for anyone to find a retail store in their neighborhood plastered with tobacco posters and signs that is less than 1,000 feet from an elementary or middle school. These retailers are often targets of local police sting operations, and those caught selling tobacco illegally to children under 18 are fined or jailed.

JOE CAMEL

The first modern cigarette, Camel, was introduced in 1913. In 1950, advertisements for Camel reported that in a thirty-day test by throat specialists, "Not one single case of throat irritation due to smoking Camels!" A testimony from a secretary taking the test said "I found Camels agree with my throat."

Curious! What does a toxic relic like Camel have to do with being cool in the 90's? Music from the 50's, 60's and 70's is history to teens today, but they accept an 80-year-old cancer stick. This is an example of the power of advertising. Advertising can transform the ancient into something new and cool.

The government saw the sharpest increase in teen smoking in 1988—the year RJR's Joe Camel ads were first introduced. RJR Joe Camel ads create the desire to smoke using visual pictures. These cartoons cause some teens to perceive smoking as less hazardous, and more socially acceptable. Studies establish that if an ad attracts a teen to be more popular or more attractive, they are 4.7 times more likely to start smoking. . . .

Why does the military draft young men when they need an army? One reason is that teens believe they will not be killed. Similarly, the threat of having a lung removed or a heart attack sometime later in life is just too remote an idea to shock kids. Research on smoking trends show that boys 10 to 14 years old, and girls younger than 21, do not respond to health messages. The health messages that have been effective in stopping adults from smoking have not been effective in stopping teens from smoking. Advertising, psychosocial motives, and peer pressures override health concerns.

TEENS BELIEVE THEY CAN QUIT SMOKING EASILY

Kids are not only missing the health warnings, they also have no clue about nicotine addiction. Teen myth: I can quit smoking any time, I am not addicted. Children don't think nicotine is addictive, and even if they did, they think it doesn't apply to them. That leads them to believe they can smoke for a few years and then easily quit. A 16-year-old smoker was asked by his grandmother "Why do you smoke? Don't you know it killed your Grandfather, and your Uncle?" His answer was "Grandmother, I am not going to smoke forever." Research has shown that about half of the teens that start smoking will smoke for at least 16 to 20 years.

THE TOBACCO COMPANIES' DEFENSE

Recently Camel ads introduced Joe's new girlfriend, Josephine. RJR spokeswoman Maura Ellis says that the appearance of Josephine in their advertising is not intended to attract children and young women to start smoking. "Not intended to attract children:" this has been the tobacco industries' defense for a decade when confronted with the accusations that tobacco advertising is designed to cause kids to start smoking. However, many tobacco company internal documents have surfaced recently, and as you now know, their actions belie their words.

Once a person starts smoking, most continue smoking the remainder of their lives. The majority of smokers say they want to quit but can't. Advertising starts people smoking, but what makes them keep smoking? The answer is the invisible drug— the addictive hook!

"There is precious little [evidence]
that advertising and promotion, on
the Web or anywhere else, increase
consumption of alcohol and tobacco."

TOBACCO ADVERTISING DOES NOT ENCOURAGE TEENS TO SMOKE

Jacob Sullum

In the following viewpoint, Jacob Sullum refutes a study that
purports to show that alcohol and tobacco advertising on the
Internet encourages youth to drink and smoke. There is no empirical evidence that advertising encourages anyone to drink or
smoke, he contends. Furthermore, Sullum asserts, the advertising cited in the study is geared toward adults, not teenagers. Sullum is the senior editor of *Reason* magazine.

As you read, consider the following questions:

1. What safeguards are needed to protect teens from the
   harmful effects of on-line advertising, according to the
   authors of the study cited by Sullum?
2. How do the report's authors define a youth, according to
   Sullum?
3. Why should parents worry about smoking-related Internet
   sites that do not advertise cigarettes, according to Williams
   et al., as cited by Sullum?

"The Budweiser frogs are particularly troubling." *Troubling* is not the adjective I would have chosen. I could see *cute,* or maybe *amusing.* After seeing them a few hundred times, *annoying* springs to mind. But not *troubling.* I am trying to get inside the mind of someone who could say that with a straight face, but it's scary in there, and I'm not sure I want to go.

THE STUDY

I am reading *Alcohol & Tobacco on the Web: New Threats to Youth,* a report issued in March 1997 by the Center for Media Education. The authors are Wendy Swallow Williams, a former *Washington Post* reporter who is now a journalism professor at American University; CME President Kathryn Montgomery, "a leading expert on television and media"; and Shelly Pasnik, the CME's director of children's policy, who also had a hand in *Web of Deception: Threats to Children from Online Marketing.* Williams et al. conclude that "[u]rgent action is needed to ensure that effective safeguards are put in place to protect young people from the harmful effects of online marketing of alcohol and tobacco."

Among other things, they recommend congressional hearings, an investigation by the Federal Trade Commission, regulation by the Food and Drug Administration, inquiries by public health agencies, and efforts by the World Health Organization and "the international health community" to develop "effective global safeguards." They never spell out what they mean by "safeguards," but it's clear they have some sort of censorship in mind. "Self-regulation is likely to have little impact," they say, "unless there is effective government oversight and enforcement."

The rationale for censoring the Web goes like this: "The increasing presence of alcohol and tobacco marketing in these powerful new interactive media could pose great public health risks, especially for young people." Yet the authors never provide any evidence (and in fact there is precious little) that advertising and promotion, on the Web or anywhere else, increase consumption of alcohol and tobacco, as opposed to increasing consumption of particular brands. They simply assume that exposure to advertising will lead kids to drink and smoke, and they go a step further, attributing quasi-magical powers to the Web. "[I]nteractivity has a hypnotic and addictive quality that some analysts believe could be stronger than that of television," they warn. "Because of the unique nature of the interactive media, many of these new forms of advertising, of particular appeal to youth, appear to be inherently unfair and deceptive."

The report is about an inch thick, but the verbose and repetitive text occupies just 35 pages in 12-point type, including a five-page "Executive Summary." The rest is notes, lists, and (mainly) printouts of Web pages. On the face of it, the Robert Wood Johnson Foundation and the Carnegie Corporation, both of which supported the study, did not get much for their money. Yet *Alcohol & Tobacco on the Web* generated a front-page story in the *New York Times* ("On Web, New Threats Seen to the Young") and received respectful coverage from other major newspapers, including the *Los Angeles Times* and the *Washington Post*.

It's not hard to see why. The CME's "major investigation," which the *New York Times* dubbed "the first comprehensive look at how alcohol and tobacco companies are marketing in cyberspace," combines three hot themes: children, drugs, and the Internet.

Exploiting parents' fears about the dangers lurking in cyberspace, already primed by rumors of rampant pornographers and child molesters, Williams et al. warn that alcohol- and tobacco-related Web sites are making "seductive appeals to youth, drawing them into an electronic world of indulgence, freedom, glamor, and fun, where smoking and drinking are the norm, and the negative consequences are never shown. In these realms of cyberspace, dangerous new behaviors can be fostered and reinforced at a particularly vulnerable period in the lives of young people." Although the Internet could be a force for good, "educational and civic services are in danger of being overshadowed and undermined by highly manipulative, intrusive, and harmful marketing methods with an unprecedented ability to capture children's attention."

THE BUDWEISER FROGS

Take the frogs. "A recent study by the Center on Alcohol Advertising," Williams et al. note with alarm (the way they note just about everything), "found that children aged 9 to 11 were more likely to be able to say the frogs' slogan ('Bud-weis-er') than that of Kellogg's Tony the Tiger"—who, the authors helpfully inform us, "is used heavily on kid's TV to sell Frosted Flakes." If you wanted to quibble, you might wonder whether there's a reason, aside from Anheuser-Busch's nefarious designs on our children, why "Bud-weis-er" is an especially memorable slogan for Budweiser. You might also wonder whether there isn't an important difference between saying it and drinking it. (In a recent survey of teenagers by *USA Today*, 99 percent knew the Budweiser frogs, and 93 percent liked them, but almost none named Budweiser as their favorite brand of beer.)

Never mind. The *real* reason the frogs are so troubling, we learn later in the same paragraph, is that they "seem to have a lot in common with college-age drinkers." As evidence for this assertion, the report cites the biography of Budbrew J. Bullfrog (the one who says "Bud"), which appears in "The Pad," part of the Budweiser Web site (www. budweiser.com). Elected president of his campus fraternity during rush week in 1989 (as a pledge!), Bud "drives a German luxury car, has memorized the entire Oxford English Dictionary and likes to hang on the beach with a hot babe, a cold Bud and a folio edition of the Kama Sutra in its original Sanskrit." Yes, that sounds just like the typical college student.

Who Is a "Youth"?

As the frog example suggests, the report is rather vague about who is threatened by Alcohol & Tobacco on the Web. What, exactly, is a "youth"? On the first page, we're told that "nearly five million youth between the ages of two and seventeen used the Internet or an online service from school or home in 1996." So a toddler is a "youth." On the next page, we learn that "the unique properties of the interactive online media . . . are particularly appealing to children and youth." So a "child" is not a "youth." On page 4, the authors worry that "[s]creening devices will do little to protect youth in college." Now we're at 18 and older. To confuse things further, on page 32 there's a reference to "underage youth," implying that some "youth" are old enough to buy tobacco and alcohol legally (over 18 and 21, respectively). Where I come from, we have another word for that sort of youth. We call him an "adult." By the time the conclusion rolls around, of course, the authors are talking about "children" again.

This slippery use of language disguises important realities. When it comes to drinking, for example, there's a big difference between a fifth-grader and a college sophomore, both of whom Williams et al. classify as helpless "youths." They call college students "one of the most vulnerable targets of alcohol marketing" and worry that manufacturers, "through the computer, . . . have a direct line into the dorm room of nearly every student." (Cool. Does it dispense beer?) This is supposed to send a chill down your spine, but it's hard to get worked up about the possibility that college students might check out the Web sites for Absolut vodka or Zima. They see plenty of ads for beer, wine, and liquor on TV, in magazines, and on billboards, and it seems unlikely that a visit to the Republic of Cuervo Gold will tip the balance in favor of inebriation, especially since *they're already drinking.* That's what college students do, wherever the legal purchase age happens to be located. But the CME's self-appointed Web watchers want us to pretend that 18-, 19-, and 20-year-olds are naive teetotalers who might be lured into a life of drinking and debauchery by images on their computer screens.

YOUTH-ORIENTED SITES

With such an elastic concept of "youth," it's hard to tell what Williams et al. mean by "youth-oriented devices," "techniques attractive to youth," or "Web sites that target youth." They say "[t]his investigation focused on the role of alcohol and tobacco companies on the Web, with particular emphasis on documenting those practices that target, or are accessible by, youth." Since *everything* on the Web is "accessible by" anyone with a computer and Internet service, this is not very helpful. "To assess whether Web sites targeted young people," the report adds, "we looked at whether the sites used music, personalities or graphics attractive to college- or high-school-aged students, and whether there were contests, sponsorship of youth-oriented music or sports events, interactive games, online magazines (e-zines) on popular culture, brand characters or other promotional devices that would interest young people."

The test for whether something "would interest young people" seems to have been formulated without actually consulting anyone young. The authors made some strange judgments. Samuel Adams, for example, is on their list of "large breweries with corporate Web sites that target youth." Visiting the Sam Adams site (www.samadams.com), one is hard pressed to figure out what they had in mind. Was it the colonial-style illustrations, the photos of the brewery, the tasting notes, the "beer education"? At the Bass Ale site (www.bassale.com), which also made the list, you can tour the Bass Ale Museum, learn about the ale's history, do the Bass crossword puzzle, or order items from the gift shop, including pint glasses, pub towels, and Dickens T-shirts. But it's Guinness (www.guinness.ie) that is most clearly going after the kiddies, offering information on the Guinness All-Ireland Hurling Championship and the Guinness "Win Your Own Pub in Ireland" Contest. The authors also seem to be under the impression that J&B, Dewar's, and Chivas Regal (all listed under "liquor companies with Web sites that target youth") are popular with teenagers.

UNDERAGE DRINKERS ARE NOT THE TARGET

Even the alcohol-related Web sites that feature games, snazzy graphics, "virtual bars," or coverage of pop culture are not necessarily aimed at underage drinkers. After all, such things are not the exclusive province of teenagers, and the hipper sites (the kind Williams et al. are apt to consider "youth-oriented") include features that suggest an older audience. The Goldschlager site (www.schlager.com) offers an interview with Joey Ramone and a review of a Pharoah Sanders album, and it has links to cigar.com and DineNet, which provides menus from restaurants in various cities. The Budweiser site has a chat room and posters of bikini-clad women, which might appeal to adolescents, but it also sells fishing vests and offers an online magazine, *The Great Outdoors*, with articles on conservation and hunting and shooting safety—not exactly kids' stuff. Williams et al. seem blind to such cues. As an example of a music event "with particular appeal to young people," they cite a blues musicians' tour sponsored by Southern Comfort. I suppose some teenagers drink bourbon and listen to the blues, but I don't know any.

Mike Ramirez. Reprinted by permission of Copley News Service.

Although Williams et al. emphasize pages sponsored by manufacturers of alcoholic beverages, these represent only 35 out of about 250 alcohol-related sites they examined. The rest consist of vendors, online magazines, and personal sites (homepages offering beer recipes, lists of favorite pubs, rules for drinking games, wine information, and so on). Presumably, "effective global safeguards" and "effective government oversight and enforcement" would need to be directed against not just Budweiser but also *Cocktail* magazine (www.cocktail.com) and Andrew Wilson's Simpsons Drinking Game (watarts.~waterloo.ca/~a2wilson/simpsons/simpdrink.html).

SMOKING SITES

Manufacturers play a smaller role in the 50 or so smoking-related sites perused by the CME. The researchers found only three sites that actually advertised cigarettes—all in German. Not to worry. "Because of the ephemeral nature of the Web, content can change very rapidly," the authors assure us. "It is important to remember that, just because something is not there yet, doesn't mean it will never emerge." They also note (over and over again) that Brown & Williamson sponsors an online magazine called *Circuit Breaker*, promoted in ads for Lucky Strike, that offers free T-shirts (but makes no mention of cigarettes). In describing the other tobacco sites—which include magazines, personal homepages, and sites sponsored by smokers' rights groups—the authors repeatedly say that, while no industry connection is apparent, the possibility of secret support cannot be ruled out.

This obsession with corporate ties is odd, since it's clearly the message, not the messenger, that bothers Williams and her co-authors. "A pervasive online Smoking-Is-Cool culture has emerged on the World Wide Web which runs contrary to the prevailing attitudes among most Americans about smoking and health," they complain. "The smokers on the Web appear to have a strong sense of community. There are many links between the lifestyle sites and the pro-smoking organizations, so it is easy for a Web surfer to find one from the other."

A Web site devoted to clove cigarettes (magnaweb.com/cloves) offers detailed information about the product's special hazards. As far as the authors are concerned, that's not good enough, because "this site also promotes clove cigarettes as sophisticated and exciting." It's "a good example of how the Web's ability to bring together far-flung people with like-minded interests can manifest as a troubling force. This site gives the few individuals who smoke clove cigarettes a forum for sharing their unique and dangerous habit." It's bad enough that dissidents dare to question "prevailing attitudes." But to have so many of them expressing their deviant views and freely associating with each other in cyberspace is just intolerable. Something must be done. We need effective safeguards.

The Smoker's Home Page (www.tezcat.com/~smokers/) opens with a caveat: "WARNING! This page may be hazardous to anti-smokers' blood pressure. Quitting now may greatly reduce your chances of moral outrage." Williams et al. should have listened. "The site has a hip, rebellious tone, and avidly promotes smokers' rights," they note with horror. "The topics . . . are very pro-smoking, with no attempt to balance the presentation of the issues." To top it all off, "In this entire study not a single Surgeon General's warning was found on any tobacco site."

Occasionally, the report's authors remember that they're supposed to be talking about the threat to "youth" posed by these distasteful Web sites. Then they throw in comments like, "Some of these sites have elements that could be attractive to youth, particularly young teenagers curious about smoking."

To show how The Smoker's Home Page appeals to "young people," Williams et al. note that the site "offers smoking-related audio, including songs from such popular groups as the Doors, the Beatles, Alanis Morissette, and the Rolling Stones." The kids today—they love the Stones. Dismayed by "the astonishing proliferation of cigar sites," Williams et al. observe that "[t]he majority of computer users are still young, well-educated, middle-class males in their twenties and thirties, just the target market cigar companies are seeking." Two pages later, they warn that "the lifestyle culture and glamor used to sell cigars could be attractive to under-age smokers." Please. Bring back the frogs.

"Isn't it reasonable to restrict or
prohibit [cigarette] advertising
when we know that at least 3,000
children are trying cigarettes for the
first time each and every day?"

RESTRICTING TOBACCO ADVERTISING WILL REDUCE TEEN SMOKING

Ronald M. Davis

In the following viewpoint, Ronald M. Davis testifies before a Senate subcommittee that the tobacco industry's advertisements portray smoking as a socially acceptable and desirable activity, while in fact, it is a health threat. Tobacco products are drugs, he asserts, and since advertising for other drug products is restricted, it is reasonable to restrict or even prohibit tobacco advertising to protect the public. Davis is the former chief medical officer for the Michigan Department of Public Health and the former director of the federal Office on Smoking and Health.

As you read, consider the following questions:

1. How does Emerson Foote respond to the tobacco industry's claim that its advertising is not directed at increasing its total sales?
2. What happened in 1964, and how did it affect tobacco advertising, according to Davis?
3. In the author's opinion, how should Congress respond to the tobacco industry's advertising and promotional practices?

From the testimony of Ronald M. Davis, in *Tobacco Product Education and Health Protection Act of 1991*, S. 1088, hearing before the Subcommittee on Consumer, Committee on Commerce, Science, and Transportation, U.S. Senate, 102nd Cong., 1st sess., November 14, 1991.

In spite of what the tobacco industry claims, and in spite of the fact that tobacco products account for approximately 434,000 deaths each year, these deadly products are the least regulated consumer products in the United States. For every hour that passes, over 50 people will have died in the United States from cigarette smoking. They will continue to die until the United States Congress acts, and acts decisively. . . .

The lack of regulation and control over the manufacture, distribution, sale, labeling and advertising of tobacco products are historical, economical, and political. They are anything but logical.

Tobacco products have been exempted from every major health and safety law in the United States, including the Consumer Product Safety Act, the Toxic Substances Act, the Fair Packaging and Labeling Act, and the Hazardous Substances Act and by administrative determination from the Food, Drug and Cosmetic Act.

The tobacco industry has the most irresponsible corporate record in America. This is an industry which still refuses to acknowledge the incontrovertible scientific fact that their products cause cancer, heart disease, and emphysema. . . .

TOBACCO ADVERTISING AND PROMOTION

I want to now turn my attention to another area of great importance, the advertising, promotion, distribution and sale of tobacco products targeted at children, women and minority populations.

These are areas which also warrant immediate action on the part of the Congress. For too long, we have listened to the tobacco industry assure us that they don't want young people to smoke; that their advertising is aimed merely at brand switching; that they don't sample or market to children; that they adhere to voluntary advertising, regulatory and sampling codes adopted in 1964; and that somehow, because we in the health community are concerned about their targeting and marketing strategies aimed at women and minorities, we are sexists and discriminatory. This is an industry which thinks that somehow they can "buy" the Constitution and Bill of Rights with their corporate profits, and then convince us that they want to protect our rights as individual citizens. One has to ask whose rights are being violated.

• Does, and should, an industry have a right to kill 434,000 Americans each year for the sake of billions of dollars in profits?

• Does an industry have a right to advertise, promote, and hand out samples of a product that is as addictive as cocaine and heroin?

• Does an industry have a right to target children with misleading advertising that suggests that the product will somehow make one more successful, sexually attractive, athletic and sophisticated?

• Does an industry have a right to not disclose to the public what it is putting in its products in the form of potentially dangerous additives?

I would say, doesn't the public have a right to be protected from these and other abuses by the tobacco industry?

To borrow a phrase from one of the industry's own propaganda campaigns, we say "Enough is enough."

TOBACCO IS A HEALTH THREAT

Contrary to the claims of the tobacco industry and its allies, the advertising, promotion, and marketing of tobacco products constitutes a health threat to the American public. These practices encourage people to begin to smoke, and to continue to use tobacco as well. We've seen it in the United States, and now we are seeing it in the Asian markets, where the industry is demanding that it be allowed to advertise and promote its products to populations, such as women and children, who historically have not smoked. The argument against the industry's ludicrous claim that advertising merely promotes brand switching is best expressed in a quote from Emerson Foote, a former chairman of the board of McCann-Erickson, one of the world's largest advertising agencies:

> The cigarette industry has been artfully maintaining that cigarette advertising has nothing to do with total sales. This is complete and utter nonsense. The industry knows it is nonsense. I am always amused by the suggestion that advertising, a function that has been shown to increase consumption of virtually every other product, somehow miraculously fails to work for tobacco products.

THE 1964 INDUSTRY CODES

. . . I want to put today's hearing . . . into perspective. In 1964, 27 years ago, Dr. Luther Terry released the first Surgeon General's Report on smoking, implicating cigarette smoking as a cause of cancer.

Fearful that their products could undergo regulatory controls or even be banned, the industry did what they continue to do so well today: they put up a smokescreen by offering up voluntary advertising, promotional and sampling codes designed to give the public and the government the impression that they are a responsible industry. For 25 years, there has been nothing but example after example of violations of these codes.

The codes were purportedly developed to prohibit advertisements and sampling practices aimed at persons under the age of 21, as well as assuring that unproved and unsubstantiated health claims were not made. I would like to submit for the record copies of the industry's codes.

In 1964, the industry readily and openly acknowledged that promotion efforts which related cigarette smoking to "sophistication," "sexual attraction," "success," "social prominence," and "athletic ability" were in fact advertisements which appealed to young people. They also stated that they would not use cartoon characters. The industry's code further required that advertisements should not suggest that a person's attractiveness or good health is related to cigarette smoking.

THE CODES ARE IGNORED

To this day, the tobacco industry has claimed that it has adhered to these unenforced codes. Advertisements . . . clearly show they have not and, we submit, never will until Congress acts to prevent this type of advertising. Yet, they have repeatedly acknowledged to Congress and the American public that the themes contained in these advertisements are in fact aimed at young people and do encourage young persons to smoke. To quote the former chairman of the Tobacco Institute, Edward Horrigan, at a hearing before Congress in 1982: "In 1964 we adopted a cigarette advertising code prohibiting advertising, marketing, and sampling directed at *young people*. . . . Each company still adheres to the principles of this Code." (emphasis added)

I think this long-standing admission of 25 long years speaks for itself. Isn't it ludicrous and hypocritical that, now faced with the prospects of congressionally mandated restrictions on advertising, the industry changes its mind after 25 years and says "no, advertising and promotion that carry such themes do not encourage young people to smoke, they merely are aimed at brand switching."

I should point out also, that the National Commission on Drug-Free Schools, in a report issued in 1990, reached the same conclusion:

> Voluntary advertising codes that limit youth-oriented images that can be used in alcohol and *tobacco* advertising are not being followed. . . . The alcohol and tobacco industries are attempting to persuade young people that drinking and smoking are socially acceptable and more attractive than they otherwise might assume. In sum, alcohol and cigarette advertising are powerful forces designed to create a new generation of drinkers and smokers. (emphasis added)

The point is that we have not really made much progress—we're exactly where we were on this issue 27 years ago. It's time we stop waiting for this industry to do what is has said it would do for 27 years. In that period of time, from 1964 to today, millions of people have died from smoking cigarettes. How many more are going to die while we debate the same old issues again and again as if they've never been discussed?

We believe it is time for the Congress to get on with its business in properly regulating tobacco products. . . .

RESTRICTIONS ARE REASONABLE

Two things . . . are clear. One, within broad limits, it is the U.S. Congress which has the authority to determine what the restrictions on commercial speech are to be. Two, the restrictions must only be "reasonable" to do everything we can to discourage smokers and non-smokers alike from taking up the addiction or prolonging their addiction when this product is killing 434,000 Americans each year.

Isn't it reasonable to restrict or prohibit advertising and other promotional practices of this addictive, killer product when it is promoted with themes that imply that with its use comes success, attractiveness, athletic ability and sexuality? Isn't it reasonable to restrict or prohibit its advertising when we know that at least 3,000 children are trying cigarettes for the first time each and every day and that cigarettes often serve as a gateway to other drug abuse problems? Isn't it reasonable to restrict advertising and promotion of these deadly products because of the tobacco industry's flagrant failure to take voluntary actions it promised 25 years ago?

TOBACCO ADS ENCOURAGE TEEN SMOKING

The Institute of Medicine sums up the accumulated scientific evidence as follows. "Portraying a deadly addiction as a healthful and sensual experience tugs against the nation's effort to promote a tobacco-free norm and to discourage tobacco use by children and youths. . . . The question is not, are advertising and promotion the causes of youth initiation but rather, does the preponderance of evidence suggest that features of advertising and promotion tend to encourage youths to smoke? The answer is yes and this is a sufficient basis for action, even in the absence of a precise and definitive causal chain."

Lawrence O. Gostin, Peter S. Arno, and Allan M. Brandt, *JAMA*, February 5, 1997.

Obviously, the answer has to be yes. By restricting tobacco advertising we are not embarking on a "slippery slope" as the industry and its allies claim. Tobacco is, first of all, a unique product in our society, one that, as I mentioned, would have been banned by the Congress a long time ago by other health and safety statutes, except for the fact that the industry, through its political might, over the years has been able to have it excluded from such laws as the Consumer Product Safety Act, the Toxic Substance Act and the Hazardous Substances Act, to name a few.

DRUG ADS ARE RESTRICTED

Secondly, it is the Congress who must carefully assess, on a product by product basis, which products warrant restrictions in advertising and promotion. . . . The Congress has already done this on numerous occasions. We are not breaking "new" ground in recommending the regulation of tobacco advertising. Congress gave the FDA the authority to regulate the advertising of drugs and, in certain instances, food—both obviously legal products.

In the case of prescription drugs (and one can easily argue that tobacco products are drugs), the Congress's and the FDA's rationale for restricting their advertising, promotion and sale is obvious. Failure to do so would encourage their use—tantamount to drug pushing. Can you imagine allowing Valium to be advertised in a similar fashion to tobacco products? I can see it now: the Virginia Slims woman says, "I've come a long way, baby. I calm down and relax with a Valium, and you should too." Isn't it reasonable that tobacco products be held to at least the same standard as other legal drugs? . . .

ADVERTISING INCREASES AND MAINTAINS DEMAND

It is easy to reach a conclusion that cigarette advertising serves to increase and maintain demand for the product. Otherwise, why else would the industry fight as hard and oppose a ban if advertising didn't promote the use of the product?

The tobacco industry agrees, but in rhetoric only, that children shouldn't smoke or use tobacco. But it knows that it is in the youth market that it has its greatest opportunities for the recruitment of new smokers. According to the Surgeon General's Report, 25 percent of high school seniors who have ever smoked had their first cigarette by sixth grade, one-half by eighth grade. We must, therefore, step up our efforts to ensure that our nation's children, 3,000 of whom try cigarettes for the first time each day, do not have access to these deadly products and are better educated about the dangers associated with them. We need to ensure that tobacco products become a part of this nation's drug and alcohol education strategies.

Clearly, we have a lot to do, a lot to catch up on, on all fronts, in our battle against this major killer. While we spend billions of dollars to fight illicit drug use, the Office on Smoking and Health's budget remains at a low level of less than $10 million. The tobacco industry spends almost twice as much in one day to promote the use of tobacco as the Office of Smoking and Health spends in an entire year.

THE TOBACCO INDUSTRY'S GAME

The tobacco industry and its allies will find fault with every and all provisions of any legislative proposal that would effectively accomplish the goal of reducing tobacco consumption in this country. They will argue that they are voluntarily implementing programs and advertising and sampling codes designed to discourage children from smoking, and that legislation is therefore unnecessary. It is, unfortunately, a game they have been playing (and playing well) for over 25 years. For years they have been winning. Winning legislative battles which forestalls significant attempts at regulation while at the same time making huge economic profits. It is the American public who has been the loser.

It is time for Congress to put an end to these unnecessary deaths.

"We shouldn't restrict cigarette ads. . . . Making tobacco a forbidden fruit may actually encourage its use."

RESTRICTING TOBACCO ADVERTISING WILL NOT REDUCE TEEN SMOKING

Part I: Ernest Beck; Part II: James K. Glassman

In Part I of the following two-part viewpoint, Ernest Beck argues that banning or restricting cigarette advertising will not reduce teen smoking. Other countries have banned smoking for many years, and teen smoking rates have remained constant, he asserts. In Part II, James K. Glassman states that although alcohol, like tobacco, is a deadly, addictive drug, advertising for alcohol remains legal. Restricting tobacco advertising will only make smoking cigarettes more tempting for teenagers, he contends. Beck is a staff writer for the *Wall Street Journal*. Glassman is a contributing editor for *U.S. News & World Report*.

As you read, consider the following questions:

1. Why are Norwegians still exposed to tobacco advertising, despite the country's ban, according to Beck?
2. In Beck's opinion, what policies would be effective in lowering smoking rates?
3. In Glassman's view, what policies would be effective in reducing smoking rates?

Part I: From "Ad Bans Abroad Haven't Snuffed Out Smoking," by Ernest Beck, *Wall Street Journal*, June 12, 1997. Reprinted by permission of the *Wall Street Journal*, ©1997 Dow Jones & Company, Inc. All rights reserved worldwide. Part II: Reprinted, with permission, from "Next Target: Liquor Companies?" by James K. Glassman, *U.S. News & World Report*, July 7, 1997; ©1997, U.S. News & World Report.

I

With his baggy shorts and baseball cap turned backwards, Kenneth Johansen is a typical 15-year-old Norwegian, skateboarding with friends near Oslo's harbor.

He's also like many Norwegian teens as he lights up and languidly drags on a cigarette.

Teenagers like Mr. Johansen, who says he smokes 10 cigarettes a day, confound, and worry, health officials in Norway. More than two decades after Norway banned all tobacco advertising, cigarette smoking hasn't been snuffed out.

While smoking has declined overall—to 34% of all Norwegians from 41% in 1975, the year of the ban—the biggest drop came in the early years after the ban was imposed. Since then, the decline in smoking has leveled off.

As U.S. officials and tobacco companies struggle to reach an agreement to settle liability cases and impose tighter ad restrictions, Norway's experience shows that simply banishing Joe Camel and the Marlboro man won't make smoking disappear. An array of factors, from spotty enforcement to alternative marketing ploys like selling branded clothing or placing cigarette packs in films, can soften a ban's effect.

"A ban is not an answer to everything," acknowledges Liv Urdal, director of Norway's Council on Tobacco and Health, which coordinates the country's antismoking programs. "If you rely on a ban alone, you'll be very disappointed. You need a comprehensive strategy."

SIMILAR RESULTS IN OTHER COUNTRIES

Norway's limited success in curbing tobacco consumption parallels that of other countries that have outlawed or curbed advertising. In nearby Finland, where a partial ban came into effect in 1978, the prevalence of male smokers decreased to 27% in 1996 from 35% in 1979. But the percent of women who smoked remained level at 18%, and the rate for Finnish teens edged up to 24% from just under 22%.

In New Zealand, 27% of adults smoke, a figure that hasn't changed at all since 1990, when a ban was enacted. And Canada's 1989 advertising ban has also had little effect: Thirty-one percent of Canadians smoked regularly in 1994, the last year for which figures are available, compared with 30% in 1990.

All this leads European tobacco companies to argue that ad bans have little effect. They note that smoking has declined in many countries, even those that haven't curbed advertising. Indeed, the percentage of Americans who smoke—about 25%, down from 42% in the mid-1960s—is lower than in Norway, despite lax advertising restrictions in the U.S.

"It's impossible to prove that [the ad ban] had any effect on consumption and smoking habits," insists Sigmund Eikeland, a spokesman for JL Tiedemanns Tobaksfabrik, Norway's biggest cigarette manufacturer and distributor.

In Norway, smoking patterns since the ban was imposed vary within the population. Among adult males, 34% smoke regularly, down from 53% in 1974, but the rate of adult women smokers hasn't budged from 32%, according to the Council on Health and Tobacco. Regular smoking among 16- to 24-year-olds also dropped dramatically, to 29% from 47%, but teens today are dabbling in "occasional" smoking in record numbers: The rate doubled to 20% over the past five years.

The mixed results in Norway reflect the complex relationship of advertising, nicotine addiction and tobacco sales, analysts say. Enforcement, cigarette pricing and cultural traditions all affect the ban's impact. For Norway, a major issue is that messages about cigarette smoking are still reaching the population—especially youth—via the global media.

While Norwegian radio and television don't carry tobacco ads, there's nothing to stop satellite and cable stations from carrying ads or cigarette-sponsored sporting events, and there are no restrictions on the import of foreign publications or films in which smoking is depicted. Norwegians who fly on SAS, the major carrier in the country, see cigarette ads in the in-flight magazine, and yellow Camel logos are emblazoned on luggage carts at Oslo airport, arguably an international zone.

SNEAK ADVERTISING

Indirect advertising isn't banned, though it is regulated. That means a Marlboro Classics clothing shop can operate—and one does, not far from Mr. Johansen's skateboarding route—but cigarettes can't be promoted there. Sporadic enforcement of the ad ban sometimes allows cigarette companies to hand out free samples at bars and clubs, which is illegal. A tobacco shop across the street from the council's office has a yellow Camel clock hanging on the door. Some companies even distribute branded items like ashtrays, matches, parasols and keychains to restaurants, says the smoking council; that's illegal, too, and the manufacturers desist after a reprimand.

Karl Lund, a sociologist at the University of Oslo who has studied tobacco advertising issues for the council, describes these tactics as "sneak advertising . . . that allows kids to remember and decode messages about cigarettes." Those messages are powerful: In a recent survey of a Norwegian movie audience, 50% said they had just seen a cigarette ad, although what they really watched was an ad for Marlboro-branded clothing, in which cigarettes weren't seen or mentioned.

TOBACCO TIME LINE

Percentage of adults in U.S. (18 and over) and Norway (16 to 74) who smoke regularly. Norway's ad ban started in 1975.

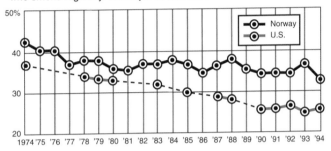

NOTE: Dotted lines signify years in which no surveys were conducted
Sources: U.S. Centers for Disease Control and Prevention; Central Bureau of Statistics/National Council on Tobacco and Health, Norway

Wall Street Journal, June 12, 1997.

Peer group pressure in Norway's schools is also strong, and the country's buoyant economy, fueled by oil-export revenue, means parents hand out enough allowance money to help kids support their expensive habit. That's important because Norway has a high unit price for a pack of 20 cigarettes: the equivalent of just over $7, compared with an average price of $1.91 in the U.S.

Although the minimum age of sale is 18, many Norwegian teens claim it's easy to buy cigarettes. Tor, a 15-year-old who asked that his full name not be used, started smoking two years ago, and uses his allowance money, despite his parents' mild objections. Tor says he knows advertising is illegal, but he sees smoking everywhere—in films, at rock concerts and at school. "It's natural to smoke," he concludes.

ADDITIONAL EFFORTS

Norwegian health officials have only recently followed the ban with education programs, and the budget for antismoking efforts was paltry until 1997. Just eight employees work at the council. "We're eight people to save Norway's 1.2 million smokers. It's an almost impossible task," complains Kari Huseby, manager of the council's Smokeline, an antismoking hot line that started in 1996.

A new law passed in 1995 could help:

Smoking now is completely banned in schools, hospitals, government offices and public places. Restaurants will soon have to allocate half their space to nonsmokers, up from one-third, and health officials are to test restaurants' air quality. Meanwhile, Norway's first nationwide education program in schools will be launched this year.

But that still might not be enough. Veterans of the tobacco wars wonder whether the only solution might be a law that forces all cigarettes to be sold in plain, gray paper. "That could be the best way to remove the symbolic meaning of smoking," says Mr. Lund, the sociologist.

II

In the summer of 1997, plaintiffs' lawyers, federal regulators, and state officials forced tobacco companies into a $368.5 billion settlement to pay for the damage to public health caused by cigarettes. The same arguments used against the tobacco industry can be used against makers of beer, wine, and hard liquor.

SELECTIVE HYSTERIA

Don't get me wrong. I'm not looking for another settlement. I'm simply trying to point out the selective hysteria that has inflated the cigarette deal and warn where the cyclone may be headed next. We encounter threats and temptations in our lives all the time, but the primary responsibility for handling them has to be our own. The basis of the tobacco deal is that we are helpless victims, lured to our deaths by evil profiteers.

Why cigarettes? Watching corpulent antismoking zealot John Banzhaf on C-SPAN the other night, I wondered, "Shouldn't he sue McDonald's for foisting fries on America's fatties?" No joke. Michael Fumento, author of a forthcoming book on the subject, says that obesity claims 300,000 premature deaths a year. And Norman Mayo, 61, of Bothell, Wash., has sued the dairy industry, claiming that a lifetime of drinking milk contributed to his clogged arteries and a minor stroke.

Says Michael Horowitz, a senior fellow at the Hudson Institute who is seeking to reform liability laws: "In these attorney general suits, if you took the word 'cigarette' and substituted the word 'sunshine' and took the words 'lung cancer' and substituted 'melanoma,' you could have a perfect case against the state of Florida." The state, after all, advertises itself with a smiley-faced sun. It doesn't warn that you have to slather yourself with sunscreen to avoid cancer.

SOBERING FACTS

To be consistent with their crusade against cigarettes, the health police have to go after alcohol. The most recent calculations by the Centers for Disease Control and Prevention place the number of alcohol-related deaths in the United States each year at 108,000. That's fewer than the 419,000 deaths attributed to smoking, but there's a big difference: While cigarettes kill in middle age or later, alcohol kills people in their prime, often in car crashes. As a result, the CDC estimates that smoking deprives Americans of 1.2 million years of life before age 65; alcohol, 1.5 million years.

Alcohol not only kills, it wounds. "In 1990," reports the U.S. Substance Abuse and Mental Health Services Administration (SAMHSA), "alcohol-related crashes resulted in 22,084 fatalities and 1.9 million nonfatal injuries."

Accidents are only the beginning. Alcohol-induced liver diseases kill 20,000 yearly. In 1993, some 708,255 patients were treated for alcoholism, and alcohol addiction was the fourth-leading cause of hospital stays for men ages 16 to 44, requiring a total of more than 1 million days of hospital care, compared with 741,000 for heart disease. The National Institute on Alcohol Abuse and Alcoholism reports that 13.8 million adults "met standard diagnostic criteria for alcohol abuse or dependence during 1992." In addition, says the NIAAA, "30 percent of suicides, 50 percent of homicides, and 30 percent of accidental deaths are associated with alcohol abuse." Two-thirds of all violent crimes are committed by perpetrators using alcohol, and 1 in 500 babies is afflicted with fetal alcohol syndrome. Alcohol, however, has one advantage over cigarettes: Even moderate smoking can kill you early, while "moderate alcohol consumption," says the *Harvard Heart Letter*, "appears to reduce the risk of coronary heart disease." Still, drinking exacts a huge toll. Enoch Gordis, director of the NIAAA, puts the total cost of alcohol misuse at about $100 billion a year.

ADVERTISING

Behind the tobacco deal was concern about children being hooked by advertising. But look at alcohol! According to a 1994 SAMHSA study, 16.3 percent of children between the ages of 12 and 17 used alcohol on a current basis while 9.8 percent used cigarettes. The tobacco agreement puts severe restrictions on advertising, under the assumption that ads entice children into smoking. But $1.04 billion was spent in 1995 to advertise beer, wine, and liquor; about two-thirds of the beer and wine advertising is on TV, while only $504 million was spent on cigarette advertising, none, of course, on TV or radio.

Should we ban beer ads? No. In fact, we shouldn't restrict cigarette ads either. Making tobacco a forbidden fruit may actually encourage its use; after all, 7.3 percent of teenagers use marijuana on a current basis (nearly as many as use cigarettes), but have you seen any ads for pot lately? High taxes and educational campaigns that stress personal responsibility would be more effective than banning cigarettes. Much of the work can be done by private groups. Alcohol-related traffic fatalities have dropped 24 percent in the past 10 years, thanks in great measure to Mothers Against Drunk Driving. Meanwhile, I was unable to find any lawyers or politicians willing to say they were targeting alcohol next. Just wait.

"Giving the government the power to
enforce [tobacco advertising]
restrictions is simply too dangerous
to the First Amendment."

RESTRICTING TOBACCO ADVERTISING IS UNCONSTITUTIONAL

Barbara Dority

Cigarettes and tobacco are legal products; therefore, restricting
advertising on tobacco products is a violation of the First Amendment, argues Barbara Dority in the following viewpoint. Allowing the government to restrict tobacco advertising is censorship
and should not be permitted in a capitalist, free-enterprise society, she maintains. Dority is the executive director of the Washington Coalition Against Censorship, cochair of the Northwest
Feminist Anti-Censorship Task Force, and president of the Hu-
manists of Washington.

As you read, consider the following questions:
1. According to Dority, what are the Food and Drug
   Administration's proposals for restricting tobacco advertising?
2. Under what circumstances may commercial speech be
   limited, according to the Supreme Court as cited by the
   author?
3. What are some positive aspects of advertising, according to
   Dority?

Reprinted from "The Rights of Joe Camel and the Marlboro Man," by Barbara Dority,
Humanist, January/February 1997, by permission of the author.

Joe Camel banned from *Rolling Stone* magazine? The Marlboro Man banished from billboards everywhere? The end of Winston Cup racing and Vantage golf tournaments? Never another Virginia Slims tennis match or musical performance?

Yes, if President Bill Clinton and the Food and Drug Administration have their way. With the noble aim of cutting teenage smoking, they have proposed sweeping restrictions on advertising and images that "portray tobacco use as fun, independent, sexy, and glamorous."

RESTRICTIONS LIMIT FIRST AMENDMENT RIGHTS

These sweeping proposals do have some opponents besides the tobacco industry—but not many. Nobody likes to be that unpopular, especially in their own circles. I know I don't. But as an anti-censorship activist, I just can't get around the free-speech limitations implicit in these proposals. Sometimes I almost wish I could, for I truly detest tobacco products. But giving the government the power to enforce these restrictions is simply too dangerous to the First Amendment.

President Clinton's strategy for imposing restrictions on commercial speech began when the FDA declared nicotine an addictive drug—which it certainly is. But it's a perfectly legal addictive drug, just like alcohol. Putting aside for the moment the substantial issue of whether the state should make the use of certain substances for individual consumption a punishable crime in the first place, these particular proposals should be carefully examined.

The Clinton/FDA legislation includes banning tobacco billboards within 1,000 feet of any school or playground and allowing only black-and-white ads without pictures in materials read by two million teens or with more than a 15 percent youth readership. The sale or display by any store of caps, gym bags, and T-shirts with cigarette-brand logos would be a criminal offense. Brand-name sponsorship of sporting or entertainment events would be prohibited. Cigarette machines would be banned from grocery stores, restaurants, and all other places where a teen might wander.

Last, but not least, the six tobacco companies whose brands teens use most would be ordered to help the FDA create televised health warnings and other educational materials at a cost to the industry of millions of dollars.

When did it become appropriate for the president or any federal agency to dictate which legal products can be advertised, where, when, and in what manner? In a capitalist, free-enterprise society (whether or not we endorse such a system), should we give the state the comprehensive power to limit free speech by censoring the contents of ads for certain *legal* products? Should the government be doing this to a legitimate industry (whether or not we think it should be a legitimate industry notwithstanding) that produces and sells a legal product grown with the help of government subsidies? And can that industry be forced by the state to pay for advertising that disparages its own products?

Despite my attempts to get around it, there's something very wrong about all this. It really sticks in my throat. As much as I'd love to see the tobacco companies go out of business altogether, these proposals reek of unfairness. Worse yet, they would impose government censorship on a massive scale. "There are serious constitutional problems with the majority of the new regulations," says First Amendment expert Martin Redish, professor of law at Northwestern University. That's putting it mildly. . . . [A district court ruled in April 1997 that the FDA may not regulate tobacco advertising.]

COURT CHALLENGES

While it is true that the courts have never interpreted the First Amendment as giving absolute protection to all speech and have given governments more leeway to regulate advertising than other types of expression, existing case law leaves no doubt that advertising is entitled to most free-speech protections.

In a 1980 ruling, the Supreme Court said that commercial speech that is truthful, not misleading, and concerns a legal activity may be somewhat limited only if the government can establish a specific interest in doing so, if the limitation directly advances that interest, and if the limitation is the least restrictive means to serve that interest.

In May 1996, the Supreme Court ruled unanimously that Rhode Island and other states cannot prohibit ads which list or refer to liquor prices, thus adding significantly to the protection historically afforded to commercial speech. Although the case (44 *Liquormart v. Rhode Island*) focused solely on liquor-price advertising, legal scholars believe it will also apply to government efforts to regulate other potentially harmful products and activities.

It is interesting that in the *Liquormart* case, the government argued that state control over alcohol is unique because the Twenty-first Amendment, which ended Prohibition, gave states the power to control liquor sales or even to ban them completely. The High Court disagreed. "Such an advertising ban is an abridgement of speech protected by the First Amendment and . . . it is not shielded from constitutional scrutiny by the Twenty-first Amendment," wrote Justice John Paul Stevens in the Court ruling.

Unfortunately, this recent ruling did not prod Clinton or the FDA into rethinking their position. "Politics is what's going on here, despite painfully obvious First Amendment problems," says Cameron DeVore, another First Amendment specialist in Seattle, Washington. How sad that even the First Amendment is fair game as a sacrifice to political expediency.

NOT THE STATE'S ROLE

I have never smoked. It's a disgusting habit, and it kills people in a very messy and painful manner. Personally, I think anyone who purposefully inflicts lung cancer upon themselves is bent on self-destruction. However, I don't believe that regulating the disgusting or harmful use of legal products by its citizens is a proper role for the state.

Underlying the impulse to control certain personal choices "for our own good" is another equally strong (or stronger) motivation: these are "sinful" products and behaviors that offend the moral sensibilities of the regulators. Certain things are "vices" which lead to sinful temptation and, as such, are an exception to commercial free-speech protections. But government has no business forcing such moralism upon its citizens.

A "KID" EXCEPTION?

Accordingly, the Liquormart decision precludes the argument that tobacco ads can be regulated for "promoting vice." So the Clinton administration is trying to create a "kid" exception to free speech. If it's illegal to sell cigarettes to minors, it reasons, it must be all right to suppress tobacco ads that underage potential customers may see.

The problem with this rationale is the same one we encounter when we attempt to keep certain reading and viewing materials away from children: adults live in the same space children do. In previous decisions, the Supreme Court has made it clear that government cannot create a situation that renders what's available in our society to the level of what is suitable for children.

Clinton and the FDA also insist that their proposed regulations meet the Supreme Court's standard of "substantial government interest to protect children." But they have to prove this assertion—and I don't think they can.

"Is the use of a cartoon character in an ad proof that you're 'targeting children'?" asks Jeff Perlman of the American Advertising Federation. "If so, what about the Pink Panther selling insulation or Snoopy promoting insurance? That argument is totally spurious."

ADVERTISING'S POSITIVE SERVICES

In addition to all the aforementioned negative reasons the state should not have the power to ban commercial speech, unfettered advertising offers customers some positive and valuable services. For starters, accurate ads convey vital information. In our modern consumer society, one cannot avoid making choices among a myriad of available products, from food to telephone services. These choices cannot be made in an information vacuum. As citizens in a democratic society, we have the right to be fully informed. After we have gathered the available information, we must be free to evaluate it and make decisions for ourselves. So the right to advertise products provides protections for consumers as well as for retailers and corporations.

SHAKY LEGAL REASONING

The administration's move to squelch tobacco advertising was greeted with general huzzahs and hurrahs, . . . but its legal reasoning is . . . shaky. . . .

Start with the obvious First Amendment problems. Until the 1970s the Supreme Court extended little protection to commercial speech, but a series of recent cases . . . have severely limited the government's authority to curtail "truthful, nonmisleading advertising." . . .

"It pains me to say this," says Laurence Tribe, a Harvard law professor who's working with the antitobacco forces, but the FDA regulations "are arguably rather too broad" to pass court scrutiny. "This is an area where there's quite a gap between what's wise public policy and what I can bring myself to say is permissible under the First Amendment."

Max Boot, *Wall Street Journal*, September 11, 1996.

Then there's the fact that, without advertising, competition would be limited and would result in higher retail prices. (It is for this reason that Ralph Nader is a strong advocate of free commercial speech.)

And, of course, the whole thing smacks of government intrusion. Surely preventing the producers and distributors of legal products from telling the public that their products exist is at least patently unfair and at worst downright tyrannical. The fundamental unfairness of the situation can be illuminated by asking a few specific questions.

What About Other Products?

What about dairy companies and the manufacturers of other high-cholesterol foods? There's certainly no question that cholesterol clogs arteries and leads directly to heart attacks and death. What about the producers of red meat? What about all that sugar? For those who believe that butter, red meat, sugar, and many other foods aren't as addictive as tobacco, I suggest they attend a few Overeaters Anonymous meetings, which is guaranteed to dispel such false notions about food addiction. Yet no one would suggest that the state ban grocery-store ads for these products.

What about sun-tanning products—or lying in the sun at all, for that matter? There's no doubt that this harmful activity directly causes cancer. Yet no one would suggest that we ban suntan-parlor advertising.

Many such other examples could be cited. In the end, it all boils down to the fact that commercial speech is no exception to the well-worn adage heard so many times from anti-censorship activists like myself: the proper response to commercial speech we don't like is still more speech. In the case of tobacco, it's already been proven that this method works. The unprecedented success of the American Cancer Society's antismoking ads—and the effectiveness of many other educational projects originated in the 1960s—tells us what we should be doing if we really want to reduce the number of new smokers. This "more speech" technique was so successful that the tobacco companies realized their television ads were resulting in ill will instead of creating customers and voluntarily pulled them off the air.

"Rather than trying to gag big tobacco, the [Clinton] administration should just talk back," says Kathleen Sullivan, professor of law at Stanford University. We all can help this educational process along by doing the same thing on an individual level.

The Heart of the First Amendment

I have always believed that understanding the heart of the First Amendment is a necessity for anyone who wants to be an advocate of free speech. You must be willing to defend the speech you hate the most just as vigorously as you defend the speech you cherish.

Sometimes it really hurts to do this. And sometimes it upsets valued friends and colleagues. But it comes with the territory.

"A total ban on all tobacco
advertising . . . could be entirely
justified having regard to the
magnitude of the public harm
caused by the promotion of tobacco
products."

RESTRICTING TOBACCO ADVERTISING
IS CONSTITUTIONAL

Action on Smoking and Health

Action on Smoking and Health (ASH) is an antismoking organization founded in 1967 to defend television's Fairness Doctrine,
which provided for televised antismoking messages. In the following viewpoint, ASH argues that it is entirely legal and constitutional to limit or ban tobacco advertising because the advertising is often deceptive. Banning or restricting tobacco advertising
would not deprive the tobacco industry of its First Amendment
rights, ASH contends, since the companies could present their
point of view through other means.

As you read, consider the following questions:

1. According to Action on Smoking and Health, what is an
   advertisement?
2. Why are cigarettes the most dangerous of all consumer
   products, according to ASH?
3. How could the impact of tobacco advertising on youths be
   reduced, in ASH's view?

Reprinted, with permission, from the leaflet *Tobacco Advertising and Its Legality*, published by
Action on Smoking and Health (ASH), October 1989.

An advertisement is an announcement, promoting a product or service, which is publicly published or broadcast and is paid for by the promoter. Congress and other legislative bodies have long recognized the potential dangers posed by many products and services and the need to regulate or even to prohibit their advertising. This viewpoint is designed to provide more information on tobacco advertising and why such advertising should have limits placed on it or be banned.

Tobacco Poses Special Risks to Children

Tobacco advertising tends to portray smoking as a socially desirable activity. This advertising falsely suggests that smoking or other tobacco use confers social skills and other graces such as being a "macho" man for teenage boys or for teenage girls it may suggest sophistication and stylishness. Unfortunately this advertising fails to disclose the health and addictive dangers of smoking.

Cigarettes are, by a wide margin, the most dangerous of all consumer products. They are the only product which is universally acknowledged to be dangerous even when not abused or when used in moderation. It is one of the few products to be found which is so addictive that many who start as children soon find themselves unable to stop. And it is a product whose use costs the American public over $100 billion each year, which is paid largely by nonsmokers.

The Federal Trade Commission (FTC) has concluded that cigarette ads tend to be deceptive, even if they contain a health warning. The Commission found evidence that the tobacco industry deliberately attempts to persuade children and others who view their ads to overlook the health warnings. This practice is accomplished by a variety of techniques which include showing smokers engaged in vigorous healthy outdoor activities, showing smokers next to sports equipment, which suggests good health, and by sponsoring sporting events.

Limits or Bans on Tobacco Advertising Are Legal

An individual state, in exercise of its police powers to promote public health, has the power to impose a total ban upon the sale of tobacco, and in the past this power has been upheld by the United States Supreme Court. It is also well established that an authority having the power to prevent the sale of a product may also prohibit its advertisement, even in instances where the product may be legally sold, as in the case of the sale of tobacco to adults in the United States.

There have been numerous instances in which the advertisement of goods or services was banned or limited although the goods or services themselves were legal. Examples where courts have upheld such state laws include bans on advertisements for casino gambling, for alcoholic beverages, for houses of prostitution, and for the use of trade names by optometric offices, among others.

SECOND-CLASS STATUS

Commercial speech, i.e., advertising, was at one time accorded no First Amendment protection. However, in *Virginia State Board of Pharmacy v. Virginia Citizens Council, Inc*, the Supreme Court let commercial speech into the First Amendment stable, if not the manor. *Virginia Pharmacy* presented a perfect opening for the Supreme Court to grant at least some protection to commercial advertising. The state of Virginia had blatantly attempted to protect drugstores from price competition by prohibiting pharmaceutical price advertising. The Supreme Court knocked down this special-interest scheme as a burden on the right of Virginia's poor and infirm to know where to find the lowest price for their medication. However, Justice Harry Blackmun's majority opinion sensibly refused to equate advertising by a merchant with the inalienable right of the lone dissenter to preach his politics in the park.

Subsequently, the Court pointedly described commercial speech as enjoying only a second-class status for purposes of First Amendment analysis: "We have not discarded the common sense distinction between speech proposing a commercial transaction . . . and other varieties of speech. . . . [W]e instead have afforded commercial speech a limited measure of protection, commensurate with its subordinate position in the scale of First Amendment values." The Supreme Court knows the difference between the marketplace of products and the marketplace of ideas.

Donald W. Garner, *JAMA*, April 24, 1996.

Since courts have upheld the rights of legislatures to ban the advertisement of legal but potentially dangerous goods or services, there would appear to be strong legal authority to ban the advertising of tobacco products including cigarettes, the most dangerous of all consumer products, which cause 350,000 deaths per year in the United States alone.

SUGGESTIONS FOR LIMITING TOBACCO ADVERTISING

A total ban on all tobacco advertising by the U.S. Congress or by individual state legislatures is supported by ASH [Action on

Smoking and Health], and could be entirely justified in regard to the magnitude of the public harm caused by the promotion of tobacco products.

Even if a total ban on tobacco advertising were rejected as being too extreme, the impact of such ads, especially upon impressionable youths, could be reduced by other methods. For example, cigarette ads could be restricted to the same "tombstone" format now required for many ads for stocks and bonds thereby providing no less protection to children and unsophisticated adults than has long been provided to sophisticated financial investors, even though the harm investors face is only financial. An alternative method might be a requirement that cigarette ads should consist only of text with no pictures whatsoever, or restrict any pictures which appear in cigarette ads besides the product itself, namely the cigarette, the pack, the filter, etc.

FIRST AMENDMENT RIGHTS ARE RETAINED

Even with a total ban on cigarette advertising, the tobacco industry would retain its First Amendment rights to present its point of view through press releases, press conferences, appearances on talk shows, and the other means which now must be relied upon by antismoking organizations. What the industry would lose is only the power to avoid the scrutiny and debate which should characterize free speech, the ability to overwhelm people through the non-electronic media with their messages, and to stifle in that media—so dependent on cigarette advertising—a fair presentation of the opposing point of view. Such activities do NOT constitute protected speech!

PERIODICAL BIBLIOGRAPHY

The following articles have been selected to supplement the diverse views presented in this chapter. Addresses are provided for periodicals not indexed in the *Readers' Guide to Periodical Literature*, the *Alternative Press Index*, the *Social Sciences Index*, or the *Index to Legal Periodicals and Books*.

America	"Selling Tobacco to Kids," February 17, 1996.
George J. Annas	"Cowboys, Camels, and the First Amendment—the FDA's Restrictions on Tobacco Advertising," *New England Journal of Medicine*, December 5, 1996. Available from 10 Shattuck St., Boston, MA 02115-6094.
Stuart Elliott	"Uncle Sam Is No Match for the Marlboro Man," *New York Times*, August 27, 1995.
Stanton A. Glantz	"The Anti-Smoking Campaign That Tobacco Loves," *Harper's*, July 1996.
John Leo	"Boyz to (Marlboro) Men," *U.S. News & World Report*, June 2, 1997.
Judith Mackay	"Taking on Tobacco Imperialism," *Multinational Monitor*, July/August 1997.
Mike Males	"Gotta Match?" *In These Times*, August 5, 1996.
Jane Pratt	"Smoking for the Thrill of It," *New York Times*, June 26, 1996.
Steve Rhodes and Leslie Kaufman	"Winston's Naked Appeal," *Newsweek*, September 8, 1997.
Ron Scherer	"A Second Wind in Tobacco Fight," *Christian Science Monitor*, July 2, 1997.
Claude Teague Jr.	"Research Planning Memorandum on Some Thoughts About New Brands of Cigarettes for the Youth Market," *Washington Monthly*, December 1995.
David Tell	"Pack of Lies," *Weekly Standard*, June 16, 1997. Available from News America Publishing, Inc., 1211 Avenue of the Americas, New York, NY 10036.
Elizabeth Whelan	"Cigarette Ads Can Become Smoking Guns," *Insight*, December 30, 1996. Available from 3600 New York Ave. NE, Washington, DC 20002.
Richard L. Worsnop	"Teens and Tobacco," *CQ Researcher*, December 1, 1995. Available from 1414 22nd St. NW, Washington, DC 20037.

CHAPTER 3

SHOULD THE GOVERNMENT REGULATE SMOKING AND TOBACCO?

CHAPTER PREFACE

On January 1, 1998, California became the first state in the nation to ban cigarette smoking in bars, private clubs, and card clubs. Smoking has been prohibited in California restaurants and indoor workplaces since 1995, and with the new law, nearly all indoor spaces in the state are smoke-free.

Proponents of the smoking ban maintain that the purpose of the law is to protect the health of bartenders, waiters, and waitresses from the dangers of secondhand smoke. A six-year study by the California Office of Environmental Health Hazard Assessment and the state Air Resources Board found that 4,700 to 7,900 nonsmoking Californians die each year from the effects of secondhand smoke. A related study shows that fully 80 percent of Californians do not smoke, and a 1997 survey found that 75 percent of Californians either prefer or do not mind smoke-free bars. Proponents argue that the smoking ban will not harm bars financially; studies of California communities that already prohibit smoking in bars show that the businesses were not severely affected by the ban.

Opponents of the smoking ban, including many business owners, contend, however, that the government should not be able to force them to prohibit smoking in their establishments. Smoking bans should be voluntary, they assert, and the law infringes on their right to decide how to run their businesses. Bar owners fear that they will lose money because smokers will drink at home or go to bars that do not enforce the law. Opponents of the smoking ban argue that patrons who are bothered by cigarette smoke should not go into bars. "Drinking and smoking go together," maintains card club owner Haig Kelegian of Oceanside, California. Indeed, surveys report that between 50 percent and 90 percent of bar patrons smoke.

The question of whether the government should prohibit smoking in all public places is just one of the issues debated in the following chapter on the government's involvement with tobacco and smoking.

| "The evidence is overwhelming: Tobacco companies need new, young customers to survive. But our kids won't make it if the tobacco companies do."

FEDERAL TOBACCO RESTRICTIONS ARE JUSTIFIED TO PROTECT YOUTHS

William D. Novelli

Federal restrictions on tobacco are necessary to reduce the high number of minors who become smokers and to counter the marketing efforts of tobacco companies who target youths as consumers, William D. Novelli argues in the following viewpoint. The author maintains that the tobacco industry's shrewd manipulation of minors and the addictiveness of tobacco demand that restrictions be placed on tobacco. Novelli is the president of the National Center for Tobacco-Free Kids, a resource center and clearinghouse in Washington, D.C.

As you read, consider the following questions:

1. How many children become regular smokers daily, according to Novelli?
2. In Novelli's opinion, what is the importance of Liggett's "smoking is addictive" cigarette package label?
3. What percentage of Americans agreed that the FDA should have regulatory authority over tobacco?

Reprinted from "Tobacco Truths," by William D. Novelli, San Diego Union-Tribune, p. G1, March 30, 1997, by permission of the author.

M arch 1997's mea culpa from the Liggett Group, maker of Chesterfields and other cigarettes, was a welcome bit of honesty from an industry so accustomed to its own lies it may have trouble recognizing the truth.

But the admission by Liggett that cigarette makers know their products are addictive and cause cancer should come as no surprise. These facts have been known to the rest of us for decades.

What hasn't been known for certain, though it has been broadly insinuated through leaked industry documents, is that the tobacco industry has intentionally marketed its lethal products to children in order to create new generations of smokers. Now we have solid confirmation of this from within the industry itself.

MARKETING TO MINORS

"Liggett acknowledges that the tobacco industry markets to 'youth,' which means those under 18 years of age, and not just those 18–24 years of age," wrote Liggett Group Director Bennett LeBow, in the statement that was part of the [company's March 1997] court settlement with 22 state attorneys general.

It should also come as no surprise, then, that among six-year-olds, Joe Camel [a cartoon character used in cigarette ads from 1988 to 1997] was nearly as recognizable as Mickey Mouse, according to a 1991 study published in the *Journal of the American Medical Association*. Or that the Centers for Disease Control and Prevention [CDC] found that 86 percent of kids who smoke prefer Marlboro, Camel and Newport—the three most heavily advertised brands.

Kids are highly susceptible to imagery—much more so than adults. A study published in 1996 in the *Journal of Marketing* found kids were three times more sensitive to advertising than adult smokers.

These facts are not lost on the tobacco industry, or on the advertising agencies they pay to create their alluring ads. Another recent survey, sponsored by the Initiative on Tobacco Marketing to Children, a group of advertising and marketing executives, found that even Madison Avenue believes the audience targeted by tobacco ads is too young to legally purchase the touted products.

A clear majority of ad executives surveyed—68 percent—said they believe targeting teenagers who smoke is a goal of tobacco advertising; 59 percent said they believe targeting teens who don't smoke was also a goal. And an overwhelming 82 percent said they believe the ads work.

Indeed they do. Youth smoking is at a 17-year high. Each day, roughly 3,000 kids become regular smokers. Another 6,000 take their first, tentative puffs. If current trends keep up, the CDC predicts more than 5 million children alive today will die prematurely.

GETTING CHILDREN HOOKED

RJR Nabisco has long been aware of the need to addict smokers at a young age. In a 1976 internal document stamped "secret," one RJR executive wrote: "Evidence is now available to indicate that the 14- to 18-year-old group is an increasing segment of the smoking population. RJR-T [R.J. Reynolds Tobacco] must soon establish a successful new brand in this market if our position in the industry is to be maintained . . ."

As RJR knew back in the '70s, the choice to begin smoking is made in childhood. Among current smokers, 89 percent picked up the habit at or before age 18. Today, the average smoker lights up for the first time at age 13 and becomes a daily smoker by age 14.

Philip Morris was also aware of the need to capture new smokers while they were still young and impressionable.

"Today's teenager is tomorrow's potential regular customer, and the overwhelming majority of smokers first begin to smoke while still in their teens," the company's researchers wrote in a 1981 internal report. "The smoking patterns of teenagers are particularly important to Philip Morris," the document concluded.

They took that research to heart, and continue to do so. Sixteen years later, during the very week that LeBow signed his historic confession, Philip Morris was staging a 10-city concert tour of rising female pop stars to promote smoking to impressionable young women. The tobacco company's record label, "Woman Thing Music," sells its CDs only in combination with two packages of Virginia Slims cigarettes—which have enormous appeal to young girls.

At the same time, RJR was launching a new Joe Camel campaign aimed at African-American youth. Menthol Joe and his buddies hover over an unseen—but implied—youngster in these ads, seductively reaching down to offer the child a cigarette. The ads plaster predominantly African-American neighborhoods and black-read magazines.

EXPOSING THE TOBACCO INDUSTRY

But the day of reckoning is coming.

Hundreds of documents spanning 40 years of industry-wide

discussions released as part of [Liggett's] settlement could show just how widespread Big Tobacco's efforts were to deceive the public and Congress about their manipulative marketing schemes and their knowledge of the harmful effects of their products.

Even if the Big Four tobacco companies (Philip Morris, RJR Nabisco, Brown & Williamson and Lorillard) succeed in blocking the release of some of these documents on grounds of attorney-client privilege, tiny Liggett can still knock a huge hole in the industry's defenses in several other ways.

Liggett has "turned state's evidence" in every sense of the phrase. In addition to agreeing to waive attorney-client privilege to release its own documents, it has agreed to make company employees and experts available to testify in lawsuits filed against its brethren.

AN IMMEDIATE THREAT TO MINORS

By executive authority, I will restrict sharply the advertising, promotion, distribution and marketing of cigarettes to teenagers. I do this on the basis of the best available scientific evidence, the findings of the American Medical Association, the American Cancer Society, the American Heart Association, the American Lung Association, the Centers for Disease Control. Fourteen months of study by the Food and Drug Administration confirms what we all know—cigarettes and smokeless tobacco are harmful, highly addictive and aggressively marketed to our young people. The evidence is overwhelming, and the threat is immediate.

Bill Clinton, August 10, 1995, press conference.

LeBow's industry-damning confession was just the beginning. A new label on Liggett cigarettes stating that "smoking is addictive" may not discourage anyone from buying them, but it will certainly make it tougher for Philip Morris, R.J. Reynolds and others to stand up in court and argue that the science is inconclusive on this subject. Liggett's cigarettes are addictive and theirs aren't? Liggett's cigarettes cause cancer and theirs don't? No jury in its right mind will believe this.

The statement should also discourage members of Congress from forging a compromise with tobacco companies, but don't count on it. Big Tobacco has a Big Investment in this Congress. They've contributed more than $10 million to congressional campaigns over the last five election cycles; in the last three elections, they gave another $11 million in controversial "soft money" to the major political parties.

Congress would do well to return those contributions and listen to the will of its constituents.

WHAT AMERICANS THINK

In a survey conducted by the Campaign For Tobacco-Free Kids immediately following the announcement of the Liggett settlement, Americans showed an overwhelming distrust of politicians who accepted contributions from tobacco companies. Three-fourths of those surveyed said politicians who accepted tobacco contributions were less likely to protect children's health.

Almost as many supported congressional hearings to look into whether tobacco companies lied about the health effects of smoking and their efforts to market tobacco products to kids. A whopping 75 percent said they believed the tobacco industry lies about marketing its products to teens.

Another statistic Congress should take note of: 73 percent of those surveyed said they believed tobacco was "an addictive drug that should be regulated like other drugs" and 70 percent said the FDA [Food and Drug Administration] should be given that regulatory authority.

Now, more than ever, it's clear the FDA rule labeling nicotine as a drug and restricting the marketing of tobacco products to children is necessary if we're going to protect American children from the greedy clutches of this $45 billion industry. The evidence is overwhelming: Tobacco companies need new, young customers to survive. But our kids won't make it if the tobacco companies do.

Which will it be?

> "The proposed [Food and Drug
> Administration] regulations are an
> outrageous and unconstitutional
> invasion of the rights of adults."

FEDERAL TOBACCO RESTRICTIONS TO PROTECT YOUTHS ARE UNWARRANTED

Thomas Humber

In the following viewpoint, Thomas Humber argues that federal restrictions on tobacco marketing and sales are unwarranted, unconstitutional, and will not achieve the Food and Drug Administration's (FDA) goals of substantially reducing smoking by minors. Humber asserts that the FDA restrictions will unfairly reduce adults' access to, and choice of, tobacco products. Humber is the president and CEO of the National Smokers Alliance, a smokers' rights organization in Alexandria, Virginia.

As you read, consider the following questions:
1. According to Humber, what is the most effective way to prevent youth access to tobacco products?
2. Why should packs containing fewer than twenty cigarettes be available, in the author's opinion?
3. Why are mail-order sales of cigarettes necessary, according to Humber?

Reprinted, with permission, from "Regulations Restricting the Sale and Distribution of Cigarettes and Smokeless Tobacco Products to Protect Children and Adolescents," by Thomas Humber, from the National Smokers Alliance website: www.smokersalliance. org/submit.html, August 7, 1997.

The National Smokers Alliance (NSA) is a nonprofit member-ship organization dedicated to fighting discrimination against smokers. Representing the interests of its 3 million members, some 20 percent of whom are non-smokers, and all of whom have certified themselves to be 21 years of age or older, the NSA provides a voice for adult consumers of tobacco products as well as those who do not consume these products but stand with those who do in opposing unwarranted govern-ment intrusion.

On August 11, 1995, the Food and Drug Administration (FDA) published proposed regulations restricting the sale, distri-bution and promotion of tobacco products. The FDA insists that the sole purpose of these proposed regulations [adopted as rules in August 1996] is to reduce the incidence of tobacco product use by minors.

The docket to which we are writing is laden with thousands of pages of closely reasoned arguments on both sides. Few will be read, fewer still will be considered, as the inexorable process of unfettered government bureaucracy grinds up principles that should be guiding the process, not subverted by it.

Neither the arguments nor the process will change several simple basic facts: There is no empirical evidence whatsoever that the proposed FDA regulations will curtail smoking by mi-nors. The principles of behavioral psychology suggest that the proposed FDA regulations may instead exacerbate the problem. Many of the proposed FDA regulations violate freedoms either stated or implied in the U.S. Constitution. Every proposed action will impact negatively on the adult consumer's access to and cost of legal products.

That minors should not use tobacco products is a belief held by most adult Americans, including smokers. In all 50 states and in the District of Columbia laws prohibit the sale of cigarettes to minors. The NSA believes enforcement of those laws—mandated as the "intent" of Congress—is the most effective solution to preventing youth access to tobacco products. The NSA believes parents, teachers and prominent role models can most effec-tively deter youth from smoking.

CUMBERSOME REGULATIONS

The NSA believes cigarettes are and must continue to be a legal product to which adult consumer access is neither diminished, denied nor rendered more expensive by arbitrary government action.

Rather than providing substantive thought to reasonable pathways to diminish smoking by minors, the proposed FDA regulations are an outrageous and unconstitutional invasion of the rights of adults, and our members know this. Confronted with the failure of the anti-smoking movement to dictate the behavior of the 50 million adult Americans who use a legal product, with the prospect of failure to achieve the goal of a smoke-free society by the year 2000, the FDA has turned to bureaucratic fiat for a solution, and our members know this. The ultimate intent is prohibition through the back doors of subterfuge and "good intentions," and our members know this, as well.

Informed of the FDA proposal by the mass media and by their own organization, thousands of NSA members wrote to President Bill Clinton, who has enthusiastically embraced the proposal of his own appointed bureaucrats. These letters form the core of the NSA's vigorous opposition to the proposed FDA regulations.

These are the voices of individual adult citizens who refuse to remain silent while the FDA attempts to control what should remain personal decisions to purchase and enjoy tobacco products. These are letters from a true cross-section of America—veterans, factory workers, college professors, nurses, teachers, clerks, sales persons, military personnel and, yes, even doctors.

We harbor no illusion that anyone in the administration has read the letters, or that the FDA will.

Many of these arguments mirror those that will be addressed in great detail by others who stand in opposition to the FDA's proposed regulations: The FDA has no jurisdiction over tobacco and Congress has specifically precluded the FDA from jurisdiction. The proposed regulations violate the First Amendment and other constitutional protections. The FDA has no useful role in further regulating a legal product already regulated by a dozen other federal agencies and a myriad of state and local regulations. The FDA proposes to squander yet more taxpayer money when it cannot even perform its current duties under the law. The classification of nicotine as an addictive drug is a mere subterfuge to gain control over tobacco despite the fact that the FDA makes no such claims of jurisdiction over other substances such as caffeine and alcohol commonly available in consumer products. . . .

COSTS TO ADULT CONSUMERS

The proposed FDA regulations require that cigarette sales be permitted only in direct face-to-face transactions between retailers and purchasers. Self-service displays, vending machines, mail-order sales and mail-order redemption coupons would be specifically prohibited.

Retail stores now receive incentive payments for self-service displays, and prohibition will eliminate that source of income. In addition, since most retailers rely on self-service to limit personnel costs, the face-to-face provision will cause an increase in personnel costs.

ENFORCE STATE LAWS

Most Americans agree that teenagers should not be able to buy cigarettes. But there are laws in every state in the union that prohibit the sale of cigarettes to minors. Wouldn't enforcement of these laws, rather than hamstringing adults who've decided they want to enjoy a cigarette, be a better solution? Shouldn't parents be in the driver's seat with regard to their children's behavior, instead of some unelected federal bureaucrat? Hasn't this silliness gone far enough?

Louise Lindblom, *National Smokers Alliance Voice*, May 1996.

Although there is no standard retail space configuration, the requirement that tobacco products be sold only from a "controlled area of the store" will effectively limit the number of brands and the quantity that a retailer may stock. As a consequence, wholesale-to-retail distribution frequency and cost must increase, particularly to smaller retailers.

These costs must be recouped and, thus, implementation of the proposed regulations will clearly raise prices of tobacco products to adult consumers already burdened by discriminatory, and in some cases confiscatory, taxation.

Taking the entire burden and cost of retail compliance into consideration, it is likely that some retailers will discontinue cigarette sales altogether. Applying supply and demand logic, a reduction in the number of stores carrying cigarettes and other tobacco products most certainly would encourage those who continue to sell the products to further increase prices. To the degree that adult smokers will also have to drive further or expend more time or energy to obtain cigarettes, there will be additional economic consequences.

FEWER OPTIONS

The proposed FDA regulations also would prevent tobacco product manufacturers from offering premiums at point of sale or from redeeming proof of purchase for premiums, denying smokers the buying power those premiums provide.

The FDA, by proposing to arbitrarily limit the number of

cigarettes per pack to no fewer than 20, would preclude the possibility of packs with reduced quantity and, thus, reduced cost, in times of recession and depression or in other situations where demand by less affluent adult consumers is sufficient to warrant tobacco manufacturers providing such product packings.

The FDA, by proposing to ban mail-order redemption of coupons, would impose a new cost on consumers who now take advantage of these savings.

If the FDA proposal to bar manufacturers of tobacco products from brand sponsorships is implemented, adult smokers and non-smokers alike will be denied the reduced-cost and sometimes no-cost access to sports, entertainment and cultural activities currently sponsored or partially sponsored by tobacco manufacturers. In some cases, especially those cultural and artistic activities that do not have broad popular appeal, it is likely that some of these activities would cease to exist altogether.

Supporters of the proposed FDA regulations no doubt privately embrace the concept that the increased cost to smokers is a societal "good," all the while continuing to publicly argue that the intent is solely the prevention of youth smoking. The FDA's real objective is transparent.

LIMITATIONS ON CHOICE TO ADULT CONSUMERS

The proposed elimination of self-service displays would require retailers to make decisions regarding the remaining space available for cigarettes. This will limit the choices of consumers, who may currently choose among a wide range of options in brand, taste, style, length, quality and price, just some of the many variables driving consumer choice.

The proposed regulations, should they become a fact, would force retailers of cigarettes to make those decisions for consumers in a marketplace controlled by federal bureaucrats, rather than a marketplace that is consumer driven.

In addition to the cost factor already cited, the prohibition on cigarette packages of fewer than 20 cigarettes will further limit consumer choice.

LIMITATIONS ON ACCESS BY ADULT CONSUMERS

The proposed regulations would ban all vending machine and mail-order sales, thus severely limiting the options of adult consumers with regard to where and when they may purchase tobacco products.

Cigarette and multi-product vending machines in factories and office buildings, in bars, restaurants and recreational facilities which cater to adults or to families would be banned, denying adult consumers the convenience to purchase tobacco products that exists for other legal products. The proposed FDA regulations make no provision for vending machines even in "adults only" or "adult supervised" locations, even though the stated purpose of the regulation is solely to prevent minors from obtaining cigarettes. The FDA's real objective is transparent.

The proposed FDA regulations that outlaw mail-order sales and redemption of coupons make no allowance for the fact that not every adult consumer is physically able to go to a retail outlet to engage in a "face-to-face" transaction. Must disabled veterans or elderly smokers who rely on mail-order transactions be penalized by the Food and Drug Administration? Must any adult individual who chooses to purchase cigarettes not available at retail for a variety of reasons (super-premium, imported, lack of broad popular appeal or marketed for reasons of exclusivity, among others) be forced to forego that choice by rules arbitrarily imposed by a government agency? The intent of the FDA is transparent.

LIMITATIONS ON INFORMATION

However one views the messages or the means of communication, the proposed FDA restriction regarding the advertising of tobacco products would infringe upon the free speech rights guaranteed by the First Amendment. Regardless of intent, to have an unelected federal government bureaucracy even seriously propose such limitations should be viewed with alarm by every citizen who regards the preservation of free speech as fundamental to this democracy.

The constitutional arguments will be thoroughly and eloquently made by others, and ultimately the courts will rule. Several points, however, should be made.

Consumers have the right to truthful information about the legal products they use. No degree of infringement should be tolerated.

Some will argue that so-called "commercial" speech does not and should not be accorded the same protection as other speech, although the First Amendment makes no such distinction. In this particular instance, however, one would impact the other in direct and significant ways. The proposed restrictions will make advertising in publications less desirable to tobacco product advertisers, and their expenditures for advertising will decrease. When advertising pages and revenue decrease, so does editorial content, which is unquestionably protected.

No degree of infringement of editorial content should be tolerated, even as a result of unintended consequences. Censorship is censorship, no matter the intent. The free speech provision of the First Amendment was written precisely and specifically to protect controversial speech—that which any element of a diverse society dislikes—from the power of the majority, from the pressure of a minority, even, perhaps especially, from the government.

RESTRICTIONS ON FREEDOM OF EXPRESSION

The proposed regulations would prohibit the sale or distribution of T-shirts, hats, jackets, coffee mugs and all other promotional items bearing the brand name, logo, symbol, motto or other identifiable characteristics of cigarettes.

The rationale for the availability of these products is immaterial. It is consumers who decide to acquire or accept the products and to wear or use them as they see fit. To deny adult consumers that right is a violation of their First Amendment freedom of expression.

Ironically, if the proposed FDA regulations are implemented, consumers may choose to wear a T-shirt featuring a marijuana leaf, a crack pipe, a syringe or an offensive slogan, but will be prohibited from wearing a T-shirt bearing the name or symbol of a brand of cigarettes which is legal to purchase and legal to consume. The FDA's proposed regulation is misguided, unconstitutional and completely transparent.

CRIMINALIZATION OF ADULT CONSUMERS

The proposed regulations define a "distributor" as any person who "furthers the marketing of cigarettes or smokeless tobacco . . . at any point from the original point of manufacture to the person who makes final delivery or sale to the ultimate user." In plain English, the FDA will dictate every exchange of cigarettes from the time they leave the factory to the time they are extinguished.

The proposed FDA regulations would thus expose vast numbers of adult smokers to potential prosecution for what have heretofore been common courtesies and everyday occurrences in the social interaction among adult smokers.

For example, the offering of a cigarette to a coworker, a spouse or a friend would be subject to FDA regulation governing "distributors," and would make sharing a package of cigarettes among adults at a bar or a backyard barbecue subject to regulation. Giving away single cigarettes would be prohibited even among adults. Sending a carton of cigarettes to a friend at Christmas would violate the regulations.

Anyone who believes the FDA would not at some point make use of the literal interpretation of the regulation has no experience with the federal bureaucracy.

UNWARRANTED BURDENS

In sum, the proposed FDA regulations would impose extremely heavy additional burdens on adult consumers who are already burdened by the high cost of taxation and by excessive limits on their ability to enjoy smoking. Higher costs to smokers, highly restricted access to legal products, less information, restrictions on expression and the possible criminalization of social behavior are completely unwarranted and will do little or nothing to achieve the FDA's stated objective.

Of course, the FDA knows that the proposed actions will not substantially reduce smoking by minors and, thus, has produced a rule to prepare for that preordained "failure"—an unspecified expansion of restrictions, and of bureaucratic power, if the number of minors who smoke is not reduced by at least 50 percent in seven years. Does anyone doubt that federal bureaucrats, left unfettered, will have the statistics in hand to broaden their reach and their intrusion when that time comes?

The proposed regulations are transparent. They are nothing more than an attempt by a federal bureaucracy to diminish or curtail the rights of 50 million Americans to purchase and enjoy a legal product.

Adult smokers do not now and should never be required to have the permission of a federal agency to smoke or to purchase tobacco products. We agreed to be governed; we did not and will not agree to be controlled.

The National Smokers Alliance, on behalf of its 3 million members, is pledged to fight the adoption of these regulations in every legal and appropriate venue. Should the regulations become law, the NSA will fight in every legal and appropriate venue to see them overturned.

"Removing tobacco smoke from the environment will save lives and reduce health care costs."

SMOKING SHOULD BE BANNED IN ALL PUBLIC BUILDINGS

Randolph D. Smoak Jr.

The following viewpoint is excerpted from the congressional testimony of Randolph D. Smoak Jr. Smoak gave testimony in support of a bill to ban environmental tobacco smoke (secondhand smoke) in public buildings. Smoak contends that environmental tobacco smoke (ETS) has significant adverse effects on the health of those who are forced to breathe it. It is especially hazardous to young children, he maintains, and the public must be educated to reduce children's exposure to secondhand smoke. Furthermore, Smoak asserts, ETS should be classified as a human carcinogen and eliminated from workplaces and public buildings. Smoak is a surgeon from South Carolina and a member of the board of trustees of the American Medical Association.

As you read, consider the following questions:

1. According to Smoak, how many Americans are killed annually by exposure to ETS?
2. Why is secondhand smoke even more toxic than mainstream smoke, in the author's opinion?
3. What are some of the illnesses that are aggravated by exposure to ETS, according to Smoak?

Reprinted from the Statement of the American Medical Association, presented by Randolph D. Smoak Jr., to the Subcommittee on Health and Environment, Committee on Energy and Commerce, U.S. House of Representatives, regarding H.R. 3434, The Smoke-Free Environment Act of 1993, March 17, 1994.

On behalf of the AMA [American Medical Association], I am pleased to have this opportunity to express our views about H.R. 3434 and the significant adverse health effects of environmental tobacco smoke (ETS), commonly known as "passive smoking." The AMA represents the physicians of this country who care for the patients at risk for disease and premature death from the effects of tobacco use. Too many of our patients are ill due to ETS. In speaking for physicians and their patients, the public health aspects of protection from ETS cannot be emphasized too strongly. The American people stand to benefit immeasurably by reducing the pervasiveness of this hazard. . . .

PASSIVE SMOKING KILLS

The need to take action to limit exposure to ETS is overwhelming. Exposure to ETS, brought about when nonsmokers inhale thousands of chemicals during "passive smoking," may kill as many as 50,000 Americans annually. It is estimated that about 35,000 of these deaths are from heart disease, 3,000 from lung cancer, and about 12,000 from other cancers. This means that *passive smoking" is the third leading cause of premature death in the United States,* exceeded only by direct smoking and alcohol. For example, the ETS cancer mortality *alone* is higher than the total cancer mortality figures from all the other environmental hazards regulated by the EPA [Environmental Protection Agency] and other government agencies *combined!* These include substances such as all regulated outdoor air pollutants, asbestos, benzene, arsenic, radiation, pesticides, active and inactive hazardous wastes, all workplace chemicals, and all other consumer products. In addition, ETS imposed upon children causes 150,000 to 300,000 cases of bronchitis and pneumonia each year, and worsens asthma in up to 1 million children annually.

The EPA document, "Respiratory Health Effects of Passive Smoking: Lung Cancer and Other Disorders," released in January of 1993, addressed some of the major health effects of ETS. This report concluded that ETS: 1) is causally associated with lung cancer in nonsmoking adults and should be classified as a Group A carcinogen, with approximately 3,000 excess deaths yearly, and 2) produces an increased risk of development of acute lower-respiratory infections, middle ear effusions, asthma, and respiratory irritation in children exposed in the home. The AMA strongly concurs with the EPA findings. We believe that ETS should be classified as a human carcinogen, and strongly support the findings of the EPA.

At least three major reviews have been published regarding

the health effects of ETS. These reports identified and analyzed many of the studies under review which served as the basis for the EPA document. The 1986 Surgeon General's report, a 1986 review by the National Academy of Sciences, and a review paper published in Britain in the same year all linked ETS to respiratory illnesses in children and to lung cancer in nonsmokers. Since those studies were published, other reports have been published that continue to affirm the carcinogenicity of ETS. The National Institute of Occupational Safety and Health (NIOSH) recently reviewed the data concerning ETS in its Current Intelligence Bulletin #54 (June 1991) and concluded that ETS is potentially carcinogenic and that *"simply eliminating tobacco use from the workplace" is the best method of dealing with this hazard* (emphasis added). We concur with these findings as well, and believe that the data is clear and overwhelmingly convincing.

FEDERAL FACILITIES ARE SMOKE-FREE

Al Gore: Secondhand smoke isn't just unpleasant, it is a risk to the public health. Our Environmental Protection Agency puts it in the same category as asbestos, radon and benzene—and those are some of the most dangerous of all carcinogens.

A Surgeon General's report found that secondhand smoke is a cause of disease among nonsmokers, including the disease of lung cancer. According to other studies, secondhand smoke also increases children's risk of respiratory infections and aggravates the symptoms of asthma.

The answer as to what to do is simple—we've got to do more to protect people from secondhand smoke in our public places and clean up the air that all of us share. . . .

Bill Clinton: I [have signed] an executive order that . . . bans smoking in all federal facilities under the control of our administration. In August 1998, every federal agency and office building, every visitors center at every national park, every facility owned or leased by the executive branch must be smoke-free.

Now, this order does allow agencies to designate smoking areas for their employees who smoke, as long as these areas are ventilated to the outside and nonsmoking employees do not have to enter them. Our federal workers and the thousands of people who visit federal facilities will now be protected from the risk of secondhand smoke.

Al Gore and Bill Clinton radio address, August 9, 1997.

The presence of carcinogens in ETS should not be in question, nor should it be surprising that such chemicals are abundant in ETS. Indeed, there is evidence that ETS is even more toxic than mainstream tobacco smoke. Mainstream tobacco smoke contains over 4,000 identified substances, nearly four dozen of which are carcinogenic. ETS, composed of sidestream smoke from the smoldering cigarette, exhaled mainstream smoke, and other components which escape from the cigarette during smoking, also contains many of these toxic and carcinogenic substances. Still other components in ETS are known to be either co-carcinogenic tumor initiators or tumor accelerants. For example, ETS contains a higher concentration of some carcinogens than mainstream smoke, including the volatile amines and the nitrosamines. In addition, ETS contains benzene, tobacco-specific nitrosamines, and radioactive decay products such as Polonium-210.

Theories of carcinogenesis generally involve repeated exposure over time to an irritant, chemical toxin, or radioactive particle leading to abnormal tissue growth that we identify as cancer. It is not surprising that ETS has been given a "Class A" carcinogenicity label, based upon what is known about the dose and time factors involved in smoke-induced carcinogenesis. Absorption of tobacco-specific smoke constituents such as nicotine and other biological markers has been measured sufficiently in ETS-exposed persons to conclude that such exposure is ubiquitous, and that the effects of the toxins in smoke do occur in nonsmokers. In a study reported in the *New England Journal of Medicine*, metabolic elements known to be carcinogens were found in healthy, nonsmoking men exposed to ETS under controlled conditions, proving that nonsmokers absorb and metabolize the cancer-causing toxins in ETS.

Respiratory Disease in ETS-Exposed Children

Physicians who care for children have long been aware of the clinical evidence linking parental smoking with a variety of respiratory diseases in children. We now teach medical students and resident physicians to inquire about exposure to cigarette smoke in cases of recurrent ear effusions, bronchitis, pneumonia, and asthma. Many studies have confirmed the relationship between ETS and these illnesses in children. Exposure to ETS has been linked with increased emergency room utilization by children for respiratory complaints, increased hospitalizations due to these illnesses, more school absences, and increased health care costs for smoke-exposed children. These problems are especially troublesome in very young children and those born prematurely or with low birthweight, many of whom may have been exposed to the toxins in tobacco in utero. Further confirmation of this was published in the February 23, 1994, issue of the *Journal of the American Medical Association*. A Canadian researcher found that cotinine is transmitted to unborn children exposed through their mothers to passive smoke.

The EPA document addresses these issues and the literature concerning childhood illness due to ETS exposure. As is the case with the lung cancer section of the EPA document, there is biologic plausibility in the assumptions made and in the conclusions reached. There are demonstrable measures of allergy (increased IgE levels among smoke-exposed children) and decreased pulmonary function in the at-risk group. Middle ear disease may be mediated by decreased mucociliary function in the Eustachian tubes similar to the effect of smoke on the lungs, or perhaps the inflammatory effect of smoke constituents.

Studies that implicate cigarette smoke exposure as a causal factor in asthma are clinically compelling. There is an increased utilization of medical care among smoke-exposed children and, as with the other illnesses studied, there exists a dose-response relationship. Airway hyper-reactivity, inflammatory changes in the airways, and the heightened allergic response by exposed children may all be implicated in this problem. Again, up to a million cases of asthma each year may be exacerbated by exposure to tobacco smoke, and as many as 20,000 new cases of the disease may be initiated annually by ETS exposure.

PUBLIC POLICY IMPLICATIONS

Finally, as advocates for patients, we must comment briefly upon what we believe are important public policy issues at stake. The public perceives risk differently when it recognizes the difference between an assumed risk and one which is imposed upon it, without the control or consent of those who may be affected. We believe that it is imperative that the public, physicians, employers, and public policymakers become educated about the problems posed by ETS. The costs to the nation in terms of human suffering and death are simply too great to be ignored. President Bill Clinton could help this process greatly by signing an executive order making all federal buildings and facilities smoke free. General public education to reduce direct smoking prevalence must also be pursued. Families with children and their physicians must clearly understand the risks of childhood exposure to ETS and act accordingly. The EPA document and the subsequent campaign developed by the Centers for Disease Control and Prevention on passive smoke exposure should have some effect in addressing this national problem by making it more personally meaningful.

TOBACCO INDUSTRY FEARS

Legislators and other public policymakers will undoubtedly continue to hear from groups who profess a "scientific" interest in the validity of this issue and who will attack it on the basis of the EPA's methodology and conclusions. The tobacco industry continues to deny a relationship between smoking and ill health of any kind. We disagree. Our experience in treating the deadly results of tobacco smoke cannot be denied. We believe that the tobacco industry fears that public awareness of the risks imposed by ETS exposure will make smoking less socially acceptable, lead to an increase in smoke-free workplaces and other public venues, and will reduce its revenues as a consequence.

We believe that the tobacco industry fears the continued erosion of its market in this country and as well, the impact of the EPA report on advertising, marketing, and litigation. Sentiment against the use of cartoon figures in cigarette advertisements . . . have damaged the industry. Tobacco use kills up to 470,000 Americans each year (direct and passive smoking combined); tobacco is the only consumer product that kills when used as intended by the manufacturer! *Tobacco is lethal, not only to individuals who use it directly, but also to those who have* not assumed its risks. Because the EPA report strengthens the data on the adverse health consequences of smoking and broadens the hazard to include the nonsmoking majority of the population, the tobacco industry and its allies will continue to oppose it. . . . The AMA strongly supports the EPA, as well as the protection of the public from ETS by regulatory and legislative means.

The AMA strongly supported the adoption of the EPA report in 1993. . . . The AMA believes that the public will be well served by continued education about ETS and action to protect it from this health hazard. . . . Removing tobacco smoke from the environment will save lives and reduce health care costs— goals that the AMA and its member physicians strongly support. In this regard, the AMA has developed model state legislation to prohibit smoking in hospitals, nursing homes, and public elementary or secondary schools, as well as other public places.

"Grown-ups in a free country, as opposed to children in a nursery, ought to be able to make their own choices [about patronizing places that permit smoking]."

SMOKING SHOULD NOT BE BANNED IN ALL PUBLIC AREAS

Part I: M. Lester O'Shea; Part II: Richard D. Berman

In Part I of the following two-part viewpoint, M. Lester O'Shea contends that prohibiting smoking in all public buildings, including bars, is an attempt to control all aspects of people's behavior. He argues that if people do not want to be exposed to cigarette smoke, they can avoid places, such as bars, where smoking is allowed. In Part II, Richard D. Berman uses an example of a mayor who banned smoking within his town's limits on the basis of protecting the residents' health to show that government has become too intrusive. O'Shea served on the Little Hoover Commission which studied pesticide residue on farm produce during the 1980s. Berman is an attorney in Washington, D.C.

As you read, consider the following questions:

1. How many nonsmokers die from cancer, according to a study cited by O'Shea?
2. What is the risk of cancer for a nonsmoker who lives with a spouse who smokes, according to O'Shea?
3. How did the mayor of Friendship Heights justify his ban on smoking in the town limits, according to Berman?

Part I: Reprinted, with permission, from "Keep the Lifestyle Cops Out of Bars," by Lester O'Shea, Los Angeles Times, September 10, 1997. Part II: Reprinted, by permission, from "Antismoking: The Outer Limits," by Richard D. Berman, Washington Times, October 28, 1996.

I

In January 1998, unless the Legislature comes to its senses, it will become illegal to smoke tobacco in bars in California. In bars, mind you, those places where people consume alcohol, in some cases to the extent that it harms their health.

One would think that in a free society where no one is compelled to patronize bars in general, or any bar in particular, such a prohibition would be unthinkable. Anyone who finds smoky bars offensive can simply avoid them.

The cute angle utilized by the tobacco scolds is to pretend that the purpose of this prohibition is to protect the health of the poor bar employees. It is remarkable that anyone can say this with a straight face.

Many bar employees are smokers themselves. And no one has to work in a bar. If you are afraid that tobacco smoke in the air will make you sick, a bar is not the place for you to work, just as if you are afraid of auto exhaust, you should not be a toll collector. If people can voluntarily enter occupations with known risks, why should they not be able to work in bars where people smoke?

Another absurdity is the supposed rationale for prohibition, the notion that a whiff of tobacco smoke in the air is a meaningful health threat. If tobacco smoke had such lethal properties, there would be very little of it around, because all the smokers would have died early.

NOT A MEANINGFUL HEALTH THREAT

According to a study by University of Michigan scientists of data collected by the American Cancer Society's massive Cancer Prevention Study II, involving 900,000 people, the death rate from cancer among lifelong smokers by age 75 was 1,250 per 100,000 men and 550 per 100,000 women, while among those who never smoked it was a mere 50 per 100,000. That's 1 in 80 for male smokers and 1 in 180 for female smokers, compared to 1 in 2,000 for nonsmokers—about 20 times as high a rate, but hardly sure death.

Note the 1 in 2,000 ratio for nonsmokers. When the Environmental Protection Agency classified tobacco smoke as a Class A carcinogen, it did so on the basis of one study that suggested a connection between tobacco smoke in the air and cancer. That study concluded that a nonsmoker had a 19% increase in the likelihood of cancer from living with a smoking spouse. In other words, if 1 in 2,000 was the risk to begin with, 1.19 in

2,000 is now the risk. Just as a 19% increase in zero is still zero, a 19% increase in something minuscule is still minuscule. And that was from a lifetime of living with a smoker.

But of course it is not really out of concern for bartenders that the prohibitionists are determined to outlaw smoking in bars.

Nor is it because the prohibitionists yearn to drink in bars but are either frightened away by fears of smoke's health hazards or repelled by its odor. Many of the tobacco scolds are also alcohol scolds, and sitting in bars drinking, with or without smoke, is the last thing they are interested in doing.

No, the reality of the matter is that lifestyle nazis are determined to force others to live in the way they think right. They yearn to stamp out tobacco smoking just as the Prohibitionists yearned to stamp out drinking. And their "secondhand" smoke terror is a powerful weapon, since many people lack all sense of proportion: Amid auto exhaust and smokestacks, they worry about people smoking near their office building's doorways.

Not all of life's pleasures reduce life expectancy (moderate alcohol consumption in fact increases it); smoking cigarettes certainly does. But so does everything from being overweight to traveling by plane or car, mountain climbing, auto racing and living in urban areas instead of in remote rural locations with cleaner air.

Grown-ups in a free country, as opposed to children in a nursery, ought to be able to make their own choices in these areas. Even Adolf Hitler, that strong opponent of tobacco, did not forbid smoking in bars.

II

The campaign to stamp out smoking in this country has now officially entered the outer limits. No longer content with prohibiting smoking indoors, antismoking activists have turned their attention to the great outdoors.

A No-Smoking Town

The mayor of a small suburban village (32 acres) of Washington, D.C., has convinced the council to declare the entire city of Friendship Heights, Md., a no-smoking zone. The mayor's ordinance bans tobacco use on almost all of the town's public streets, sidewalks and parks. The regulation goes far beyond protecting non-smokers from exposure to secondhand smoke. It stops people from smoking outdoors—which has no consequences for anyone except the individual smoker. The village of Friendship Heights now has the most stringent anti-smoking law in the nation, and will no doubt serve as a model for others.

To his credit, the mayor didn't try to hide his motives for the ban by claiming it was necessary for litter control or pollution abatement (as others have done). The mayor claims that for health reasons he's trying to "persuade people to stop smoking with a little gentle pressure." Woe be to the good people of Friendship Heights if the mayor becomes concerned about the weight or drinking habits of the villagers. He could easily decide that a "little gentle pressure" is needed to wean people away from fatty foods and alcohol.

© Bob Lang Editorial Services. Reprinted by permission.

The mayor's propensity to treat his constituents as patients has serious consequences for more than his little fiefdom. Just as consumers of tobacco and liquor are being labeled by the fringe groups as users of "drug delivery systems," those who dine out at restaurants are coming under increasing scrutiny for eating "deadly doses" of fat and cholesterol.

A critic of the mayor's action asked if the village council "will next attempt to forbid people from eating hot dogs on village sidewalks because they are high in cholesterol and have little nutritional value?" That concern is not so far-fetched. The Center for Science in the Public Interest (CSPI) has already taken their complaints about the "dangers" of restaurant food to the public. In the past they have scared off patrons from eating certain types of food; now they are scolding restaurants about serving too much food. Most recently, they've condemned casual dining restaurants, saying, "It's high time that the industry began to bear some responsibility for its contribution to obesity, heart disease and cancer."

The attack by CSPI may provoke a big yawn by most of the public. After all, CSPI issues outrageous statements about food on a regular basis. However, their latest assault builds on the growing sentiment that it is O.K. to regulate personal behavior in order to "help" or "protect" people from themselves. It is precisely the sentiment behind the mayor's actions.

A GOOD-FOR-YOU LAW?

Many villagers dismissed the mayor's argument that secondhand smoke in an outdoor setting is a threat to their health. Some cited the dangers of car exhaust fumes as a bigger problem. But, the mayor won the council over as he successfully couched the ban in terms that made it more difficult to argue with—after all, what's a little inconvenience if it is good for you?

The passage of this law combined with the growing "eat your vegetables" mentality of consumer groups creates an environment where government believes it is justified in regulating broader personal behaviors which have no "health" consequences for anyone except the individual consumer. In this picture, the differences between a cheeseburger and a cigarette disappear.

The mayor of Friendship Heights cited the U.S. Constitution as justification for his smoking ban. His interpretation of promoting the "general welfare" will likely be embraced by many others.

What happened in Friendship Heights is yet another wake-up call for all of us. We can no longer afford to treat the workings of town councils and local boards of health as a spectator sport. These little skirmishes have a "big picture" fall-out effect on our personal freedoms and how we are "allowed" to live our lives. While federal and state regulators continue to worm their way into our personal lives, we need to make time to participate in local government. If you don't believe it, ask the folks in Friendship Heights.

| "A [cigarette] tax hike would continue to discourage smoking for successive generations of young people."

TOBACCO TAXES SHOULD BE INCREASED

Michael Grossman and Frank J. Chaloupka

Increasing taxes on cigarettes is an effective way to reduce teen smoking because teenagers are especially sensitive to price, contend Michael Grossman and Frank J. Chaloupka in the following viewpoint. A reduction in teen smoking would also lessen the peer pressure to smoke felt by many teens, the authors argue. Moreover, they maintain, since nearly all smokers start as teenagers, increasing taxes would result in a reduction of older smokers in the long run. Grossman is a distinguished professor of economics at the City University of New York Graduate School, program director of health economics, and a research associate at the National Bureau of Economic Research. Chaloupka is an associate professor of economics at the University of Illinois at Chicago and a research associate at NBER.

As you read, consider the following questions:

1. According to the authors, what percentage of smokers began smoking before age 18?
2. What evidence do Grossman and Chaloupka give to support their theory that the number of teenage smokers is sensitive to the price of cigarettes?
3. What three caveats are required when evaluating the benefits of a cigarette tax increase, according to the authors?

Reprinted from "Cigarette Taxes: The Straw to Break the Camel's Back," by Michael Grossman and Frank J. Chaloupka, Public Health Reports, July/August 1997, a publication of the U.S. Public Health Service.

These are not good times for the U.S. cigarette industry. For decades, policy makers and consumer activists have unsuccessfully attempted to rein in the tobacco industry. Now, new legal strategies are bearing fruit, more stringent regulations regarding the marketing and sales of cigarettes are being implemented. A large cigarette tax complements the gains made on other fronts by making cigarettes less desirable to teenagers, the next generation of addicts. . . .

Numerous studies have shown that roughly 90% of smokers begin the habit as teenagers. Each day, approximately 6000 youths try a cigarette for the first time, and about half of them become daily smokers. Among people who have ever smoked daily, 82% began smoking before age 18. Thus, cigarette control policies that discourage smoking by teenagers may be the most effective way of achieving long-run reductions in smoking in all segments of the population.

The upward trend in teenage smoking in the 1990s is alarming to public health advocates. Between 1993 and 1996 the number of high school seniors who smoke grew by 14%. At the same time the number of tenth grade smokers rose by 23%, and the number of eighth grade smokers rose by 26%.

The FDA [Food and Drug Administration] regulations approach the problem of youth smoking by curtailing access to cigarettes and attempting to reduce the appeal of cigarettes by putting limits on cigarette advertising. Increased taxation, which results in higher prices, is another means to accomplish the goal of discouraging young people from smoking. . . .

WHY TAXES WORK

There are strong logical reasons for expecting teenagers to be more responsive to the price of cigarettes than adults. First, the proportion of disposable income that a youthful smoker spends on cigarettes is likely to exceed the corresponding proportion of an adult smoker's income. Second, peer pressure effects are much more important in the case of youth smoking than in the case of adult smoking. Interestingly, peer pressure has a positive multiplying effect when applied to teenage smokers: a rise in price curtails youth consumption directly and then again indirectly through its impact on peer consumption (if fewer teenagers are smoking, fewer other teenagers will want to emulate them). Third, young people have a greater tendency than adults to discount the future.

The "full" price to an individual of a harmful smoking addiction is the price of cigarettes plus the monetary and emotional costs to the individual of future adverse health effects. The importance and value placed on these future health effects varies among individuals and especially with age. Gary S. Becker, Michael Grossman, and Kevin Murphy have shown that young people are more responsive to the price of cigarettes than adults because they give little weight to the future, while adults are more sensitive to perceived or known future consequences. Young people may underestimate the health hazards of and the likelihood that initiation of this behavior leads to long-term dependency. And, even when fully informed, teenagers have a tendency to give a great deal of weight to present satisfaction and very little weight to the future consequences of their actions.

Becker and Casey B. Mulligan argue that children become more future oriented as the result of an investment process. Many of the activities of parents and schools can be understood as attempts to make children care more about the future. Some parents and schools succeed in these efforts, but others do not. These failures are particularly troublesome because of the two-way causality between addiction and lack of a future orientation. People who discount the future more heavily are more likely to become addicted to nicotine and other substances. And the adverse health consequences of these substances make a future orientation even less appealing.

THE DANGERS OF SMOKING

Consumers are not unaware of the dangers of smoking. A survey by W. Kip Viscusi suggests that both smokers and nonsmokers overestimate, not underestimate, the probability of death and illness from lung cancer due to tobacco. Teenagers, who have less information than adults, actually attach much higher risks to smoking than the rest of the population. Other risks of cigarette smoking, including the risk of becoming addicted, may, however, be underestimated.

Cigarette smokers harm others (external costs) in addition to harming themselves (internal costs). The ignored internal costs of smoking can interact with the external costs. A striking example is smoking by pregnant teenage women, who may engage in this behavior because they heavily discount the future consequences of their current actions. Pregnant women who smoke impose large external costs on their fetuses. Numerous studies show that these women are more likely to miscarry and to give birth to low birth weight infants. Some of these infants die within the first month of life. More require extensive neonatal intensive care and suffer long-term impairments to physical and intellectual development.

The conventional wisdom argues that people who are addicted to nicotine are less sensitive to price than others. Therefore, adults should be less responsive to price than young people because adult smokers are more likely to be addicted to nicotine and, if so, are likely to be more heavily addicted or to have been addicted for longer periods of time. The conventional wisdom that addicted smokers are less sensitive to price has been challenged in a formal economic model of addictive behavior developed by Becker and Murphy, which shows that a price increase can have a cumulative effect over time. . . .

THE EVIDENCE

Suggestive evidence of the responsiveness of teenage smoking to the price of cigarettes can be found in recent upward trends in smoking. In April 1993, the Philip Morris Companies cut the price of Marlboro cigarettes by 40 cents. Competitors followed suit. Marlboros are popular among teenagers: 60% reported that Marlboro was their brand of choice in 1993, while Marlboro had an overall market share of 23.5% in the same year. In 1993, 23.5% of teenagers in the eighth, tenth, and twelfth grades smoked. In 1996, 28.0% of the students in these grades smoked; this represented a 19% increase over a three-year period. Yet during this period, the number of smokers ages 18 years and older remained the same. Some attribute this increase in teenage smoking to a broad range of social forces thought to be associated with increases in other risky behaviors by teenagers, especially the use of marijuana. But we attribute it to a fall in cigarette prices: between 1993 and 1996 the real price of a pack of cigarettes (the cost of a pack of cigarettes in a given year divided by the Consumer Price Index for all goods for that year) fell by 13%.

More definitive evidence of the price sensitivity of teenage smoking can be found in two NBER [National Bureau of Economic Research] studies that used large nationally representative samples of thousands of young people between the ages of 12 and 17. These studies capitalized both on the substantial variation in cigarette prices across states (primarily because of different state excise tax rates on this good) and on other state-specific factors such as parents' education and labor market status that may affect the decision to smoke and the quantity of cigarettes consumed. The findings of a 1981 study by Grossman, Eugene M. Lewit, and Douglas Coate . . . were used by the news media throughout the 1980s and early 1990s to project the effects of Federal excise tax hikes. The authors' 1996 study has been cited by Senators Orrin Hatch and Ted Kennedy as evidence that a major benefit of [a] tax increase . . . would be to discourage youth smoking.

ADDITIONAL STUDIES

The Grossman et al. 1981 study used data from Cycle III of the U.S. Health Examination Survey, a survey of almost 7000 young people between the ages of 12 and 17 conducted between 1966 and 1970 by the National Center for Health Statistics. The authors found that a 10% increase in the price of cigarettes would reduce the total number of youth smokers by 12%. Yet teenagers who already smoked proved much less sensitive to price: a 10% increase in price would cause daily consumption to fall by only 2%.

In our 1996 study, we used data from the 1992, 1993, and 1994 surveys of eighth, tenth, and twelfth grade students conducted by the Institute for Social Research at the University of Michigan as part of the Monitoring the Future Project. Taken together, these three nationally representative samples included approximately 150,000 young people. We found that a 10% increase in price would lower the number of youthful smokers by 7%, a somewhat smaller effect than the 12% projected in the 1981 study. Consumption among smokers, however, would decline by 6%, which is three times larger than the decline projected in the 1981 study.

Comparable studies of adults have found smaller effects of a projected 10% price increase. In a 1982 study of people age 20 years and older, Lewit and Coate reported that a 10% rise in price would cause the number of adults who smoke to fall by 3% and a decline of 1% in the number of cigarettes smoked per day by those who smoke. In a 1991 study of adult smokers, Jeffrey Wasserman et al. found that a 10% increase in price would cause the number who smoked to fall by 2% and the number of cigarettes smoked per day to fall by 1% while in a 1995 study William N. Evans and Matthew C. Farrelly found declines of 1% in both categories. Based on the most recent estimates, a 10% increase in the price of cigarettes would reduce the number of teenagers who smoke by 7% while it would reduce the number of adults who smoke by only 1%. Daily consumption of teenage smokers would fall by 6%, while daily consumption of adult smokers would fall by 1%.

PRICE INCREASES AS A POLICY TOOL

[A] proposed 43-cent cigarette tax hike . . . would, if fully passed on to consumers, raise the price of a pack of cigarettes by approximately 23%. According to our 1996 study, the number of teenage smokers would fall by approximately 16% and the number of cigarettes consumed by teenage smokers would decline by approximately 14%. Some of these smokers might compensate for a reduction in the number of cigarettes smoked by switching to higher nicotine and tar brands, inhaling more deeply, or reducing idle burn time. These factors, while representing a pubic health concern, are not relevant in evaluating the effect of an excise tax hike on whether an individual chooses to smoke at all.

U.S. CIGARETTE TAXES ARE $1.00 LESS THAN IN 14 DEVELOPED COUNTRIES

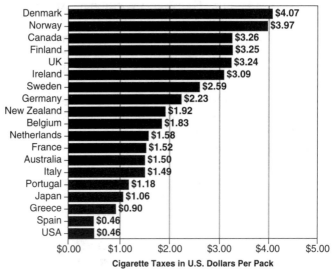

Cigarette Taxes in U.S. Dollars Per Pack

Foreign taxes expressed in U.S. dollars are approximate due to currency fluctuations.

Coalition on Smoking OR Health, 1993.

Since very few smokers begin smoking after the ages of 20, these relatively large reductions in the total number of teenage smokers imply that excise tax increases are very effective ways to prevent the onset of a habitual behavior with serious future health consequences. A 16% decline in the number of young smokers associated with a 43-cent tax hike translates into over 2.6 million fewer smokers in the current cohort of 0 to 17-year-olds. Using a common estimate that one in three smokers dies prematurely from smoking-related illnesses, we can calculate that over time a real (adjusted for inflation) 43-cent tax increase would reduce smoking-related premature deaths in this cohort by over 850,000. And larger tax increases would result in even bigger reductions in the number of young smokers and the number of premature deaths.

A tax hike would continue to discourage smoking for successive generations of young people and would gradually affect the smoking levels of older age groups as the smoking-discouraged cohorts move through the age spectrum. Over a period of several decades, aggregate smoking and its associated detrimental health effects would decline substantially.

The effect of a price or tax hike also grows over time because of the addictive nature of smoking: a small reduction in current cigarette consumption by smokers due to a tax hike would decrease consumption in all future years to follow. Becker, Grossman, and Murphy have estimated that each 10% rise in price causes the number of cigarettes consumed by a fixed population (number of smokers multiplied by cigarettes consumed per smoker) to fall by 4% after one year and by as much as 8% after approximately 20 years.

CAVEATS

Several caveats are required in evaluating the benefits of a tax hike. First, for a cigarette tax increase to continue at the same level in real terms, it would have to be indexed to the rate of inflation. The same objective could hypothetically be accomplished by converting to an *ad valorem* cigarette excise tax system under which the cigarette tax is expressed as a fixed percentage of the manufacturer's price. The latter approach has one limitation: the Congressional Budget Office points out that it might induce manufacturers to lower sales prices to company-controlled wholesalers to avoid part of the tax.

Second, Robert L. Ohsfeldt, R.G. Boyle, and E.I. Capilouto have reported that the number of males between the ages of 16 and 24 who use smokeless tobacco would rise by approximately 12% if a state excise tax rate on cigarettes rose by 10%. Some would view such an increase with alarm because smokeless tobacco increases the risks of oral cancer and other oral diseases. On the other hand, Brad Rodu argues that these elevated risks are very small and are more than offset by reductions in cigarette-related cancers and heart disease. The substitution of smokeless tobacco for cigarettes could be discouraged by raising the Federal excise tax on smokeless tobacco. But this would raise the cost of a safer nicotine delivery system than cigarettes and could be viewed as an unfair penalty on those who cannot give up their addiction.

Third, in strictly financial terms, we would expect a tax hike to yield higher rates of return in the short run than in the long run because of its cumulative effect in reducing smoking. The Becker et al. study implies that a Federal excise tax rate on cigarettes of approximately $1.00 a pack would maximize long-run Federal revenue from the tax at roughly $13.3 billion annually approximately 10 to 20 years after the new rate is in effect—only $7.6 billion more than the revenue from today's 24-cent tax. . . .

The gap between long-run and short-run tax yields highlights a danger of justifying a cigarette tax increase to achieve goals other than reductions in smoking. For a while, public health advocates can have their cake and eat it too. But after a number of years, the large cumulative reduction in smoking would take a big bite out of the tax revenues initially generated by the tax hike. One would hardly like to see the development of a situation in which fiscal needs create pressure on the government to encourage smoking or at least not discourage it. The extensive advertising campaigns conducted by state-run lotteries are examples of the danger of the government becoming too dependent on revenue from a harmful addiction.

| "A dramatic jump in the [cigarette] tax. . . . could . . . lead to a black market in tobacco."

TOBACCO TAXES SHOULD NOT BE INCREASED

Stephen Gold

For many years, Congress has proposed tax increases on cigarettes to fund various health programs and to encourage people to quit smoking. In the following viewpoint, Stephen Gold argues that while a $2 tobacco tax would price cigarettes out of the reach of some smokers, many others would turn to black market cigarettes instead. Tobacco is too addictive for a prohibitive tax increase to persuade people to give it up. Gold is the communications director at the Tax Foundation in Washington, D.C.

As you read, consider the following questions:

1. What is the "elasticity of demand," as explained by Gold?
2. What evidence does the author present to support his contention that a dramatic increase in the federal tobacco tax would lead to black marketeering?
3. According to economists cited by Gold, how could a 100 percent price increase affect cigarette sales?

Reprinted, with permission, from "Are We Heading for an Era of Cigarette Prohibition?" by Stephen Gold, *Washington Times*, February 18, 1994.

Two darkly dressed men, coat collars raised around their necks, scurry along a dimly lit street in Georgetown. Every block or so, they look over their shoulders to make sure no one is following. Suddenly they turn into a driveway, unlock a side gate, and duck into the backyard and down a flight of stairs to a basement door.

One of the men taps out a secret knock on the door. It sounds like the beat to "Shave and a Haircut." The door opens, and a great cloud of smoke envelops the visitors. They inhale deeply, and smile.

They've entered the world of the cigarette speakeasy.

Of course, there are no cigarette speakeasies today. But two Members of Congress—Sen. Paul Wellstone and Rep. Jim McDermott—introduced health care reform legislation that would raise the federal excise on a pack of cigarettes from the current 24 cents to $2. [The legislation did not pass.] This mirrors a proposal by an impressive coalition of health care groups, past surgeons general, and former President Jimmy Carter, which called for a $2 federal excise tax as well as more stringent controls on the sales and advertising of cigarettes.

Such a dramatic jump in the tax, making a pack of cigarettes prohibitively expensive for many Americans, could well have the same practical effect on smokers as an outright ban. That, of course, is what a lot of reformers want. But could such action also lead to a black market in tobacco? And with a black market, could the opening of secret speakeasies reserved for illicit cigarette smoking be far behind?

THE ECONOMICS OF A TAX INCREASE

Let's look at the economics. Whenever the price of a product rises or falls, consumption of the product tends to shift inversely, a reaction economists call the "elasticity of demand." A modest rise in the price of cigarettes, then, could be expected to lead to a modest drop in the number of cigarettes consumed. This is exactly what health care specialists hope for when they call for higher excise taxes. In fact, based on traditional consumption patterns, raising the federal tax from 24 cents to $2 would reduce the number of packs consumed annually by about 36 percent—from 25.4 billion packs to 16.3 billion packs.

But a 733 percent hike in the federal excise on cigarettes isn't any ordinary levy. It would almost double the average price of a pack of cigarettes in the U.S. from $2.25 to $4.25. As Tax Foundation Senior Economist Arthur Hall relates, "Such a large tax might dramatically change the historical consumer reaction to past price increases." Normally, when trying to project consumption patterns in cigarettes, analysts use a standard formula for small price increases: every 1 percent rise in price will generate a 0.4 percent decrease in consumption. But if prices shoot through the roof, Dr. Hall says, a 100 percent price increase "could plausibly result in an almost 90 percent decrease in the number of packs consumed"—a virtual free fall from 25.7 billion packs to 2.7 billion packs consumed annually. At least, that's all federal officials would be able to measure.

The rest of the cigarettes would likely be smoked "underground."

That's because tobacco isn't any ordinary product. Like alcohol, it's highly lucrative business. More to the point, tobacco has a fiercely loyal consumer base, and unlike other consumer products, there are no practical alternatives to it. For example, if you raise the price of coffee dramatically, caffeine-dependent consumers would be angry but they'd simply start drinking more tea or cola. But jack up the price of cigarettes, and where would nicotine addicts turn? As the guy with the black eye used to say on the old Tareyton cigarette commercials, most smokers would probably rather fight than switch.

In fact, when state excise taxes on cigarettes have been hiked sharply, a modified form of black marketeering has indeed evolved. In a study published by the Tax Foundation in 1992, the accounting firm of KPMG Peat Marwick found that cross-border

---

THE CIGARETTE TAX HIKE: WHO PAYS?

In 1997, Congress approved a 10-cent-per-pack excise tax increase to take effect in 2000, with another 5-cent increase in 2002. These taxes will affect mostly poor and low-income smokers.

Adjusted Gross Income	Share of Tax Burden	Five-Year Total (millions)
under $15,000	34.0%	$1,756
$15,000 to $25,000	17.2%	891
$25,000 to $35,000	16.8%	866
$35,000 to $45,000	6.9%	357
$45,000 to $60,000	8.8%	454
$60,000 to $75,000	6.1%	314
$75,000 to $100,000	4.1%	211
$100,000 to $200,000	4.7%	245
$200,000 or more	1.4%	73

Tax Foundation, *Reason*, November 1997.

shopping in relatively low-taxed states and even smuggling are quite prevalent among consumers in states with high cigarette prices or excise taxes. For instance, many smokers in New York City—which tacks on a 13 cents citywide levy to the state's 56 cents and the federal government's 24 cent tax—not only cross into neighboring counties in New York and New Jersey to buy lower-priced cigarettes, but they also purchase cartons from low-tax states like Virginia to avoid their local tax burden.

When Massachusetts' cigarette excise doubled from 25 cents to 51 cents in 1993, sales were projected to fall off by about 25 percent. Did that mean people would stop smoking? Some might have chosen that route. But two-thirds of this decline in sales was expected to be due to increased cross-border shopping, into neighboring New Hampshire and Vermont. Another eight percent was expected to come from increased smuggling.

So what happens when state differentials in cigarette prices become moot because of a skyrocketing federal excise? Health care officials hope smokers will give up their habits and turn to sucking Lifesavers.

A MONEY-MAKING PRODUCT

But they underestimate the influential role tobacco plays in our society. Not only is it addicting to users, profits from tobacco sales are highly alluring to farmers and manufacturers. Total gross national product for the tobacco industry hovered around $18 billion in 1992, yet there were only 153,000 people helping raise tobacco in the fields and another 40,000 involved in turning it into consumer product. That adds up to a cool average of $93,000 per employee.

Of course, those neat sales wouldn't last if tobacco prices rose dramatically and people gave up smoking. Then again, who says they have to stop? A strong demand for the product and the lure of money will continue to exist, and the infrastructure is already in place that would allow organized crime to expand in this area. Farmers will simply harvest a certain amount of their tobacco crop for the black market. Underground cigarette manufacturers, like the Prohibition-era whiskey producers before them, will pop up in various locales to surreptitiously buy tobacco leaves from agreeable farmers. The manufacturers, in turn, will sell their product to "retailers," who will market the untaxed bootleg cigarettes in speakeasies.

Go ahead and call it a foolish scenario. That's what the Anti-Saloon League thought eight decades ago, on the verge of Prohibition.

PERIODICAL BIBLIOGRAPHY

The following articles have been selected to supplement the diverse views presented in this chapter. Addresses are provided for periodicals not indexed in the *Readers' Guide to Periodical Literature*, the *Alternative Press Index*, the *Social Sciences Index*, or the *Index to Legal Periodicals and Books*.

Andrew M. Budai	"Make Way for Tobacco Cops and Beware," *Insight*, November 4, 1996. Available from 3600 New York Ave. NE, Washington, DC 20002.
Rebecca Clay	"Unfriendly Fumes," *Environmental Health Perspectives*, November 1996. Available from Superintendent of Documents, PO Box 371954, Pittsburgh, PA 15250-7954.
Bill Clinton	"Excerpts from Clinton News Conference on His Tobacco Order," *New York Times*, August 11, 1995.
John Corry	"A Freedom Lover in Mesa, Arizona," *American Spectator*, January 1997.
Economist	"An Anti-Smoking Wheeze," August 19, 1995.
Mike France	"Costlier Smokes, Cleaner Lungs?" *Business Week*, October 6, 1997.
Stephen Goode	"Call It a 'Stinking Weed,' Just Don't Try to Ban It," *Insight*, June 16, 1997.
Richard B. Heyman	"Teenage Smoking: More Laws Are Needed," *World & I*, December 1995. Available from 3600 New York Ave. NE, Washington, DC 20002.
Thomas Humber	"Kids Can Think for Themselves," *World & I*, December 1995.
Matthew Miller	"Clean Lungs at a Price," *U.S. News & World Report*, July 7, 1997.
Randolph D. Smoak Jr.	"The AMA's Tobacco Fight," *Vital Speeches of the Day*, February 1, 1996.
Jacob Sullum	"Imbalancing Act," *National Review*, January 23, 1995.
Paul R. Torrens	"Watch the Nicotine," *America*, October 11, 1997.

CHAPTER 4

SHOULD TOBACCO COMPANIES BE SANCTIONED?

CHAPTER PREFACE

In 1997, INFACT, a national corporate watchdog organization, went on a city-to-city tour to display its "Face the Faces" public education project, a collection of photographs of people who had contracted smoking-related illnesses. The goal of the photographic presentation was "to put a human face" on the three million worldwide deaths caused annually by smoking and to reveal the "lives broken and lost due to [the tobacco] industry's deadly practices." One photograph depicted Jeanne, a Florida woman dying of smoking-related emphysema, who wrote: "My mother and brother both had cancer of the jaw and my father (62 years), my husband (46 years), and son (29 years) all died of heart attacks that I've been told would probably not have happened if they were not heavy smokers." Jeanne and groups such as INFACT believe that tobacco companies should be held financially liable for these deaths. To accomplish this, several individuals and states have sued cigarette manufacturers for smoking-related health damages. They argue that the tobacco industry intentionally misled the public by understating the dangers of tobacco use. Such deliberate misinformation, they contend, is the reason why many people choose to smoke.

Others, including University of California business professor Richard B. McKenzie, maintain that tobacco companies are not responsible for individuals' decisions to smoke. In McKenzie's opinion, "The fact that millions of people have kicked the habit indicates that a degree of choice plays a role in people's decisions to smoke. Moreover, addicted smokers were not always so: At some point, they had a choice about whether to go down the addictive path of smoking." Several commentators argue, furthermore, that the public has long been aware of the dangers of tobacco use despite cigarette companies' tendency to downplay the hazards of their product. Smokers know the habit is dangerous, claims syndicated columnist Stephen Chapman: "Smokers smoke because they value the satisfactions of smoking more than they fear its hazards."

The question of whether the tobacco industry should be held liable for health damages is one of the controversies examined by the authors of the following chapter.

| "The tobacco industry's deception . . .
| had effects, and these effects hurt the
| people deceived."

THE TOBACCO INDUSTRY IS RESPONSIBLE FOR ENCOURAGING SMOKING

Andrew Bard Schmookler

Several states and individuals have sued tobacco companies for health damages claimed to be caused by cigarette smoking. In response to these lawsuits, the tobacco industry has proposed a global settlement which would include tobacco-industry payments to compensate states for the costs of treating smoking-related illnesses and immunity from future lawsuits. In the following viewpoint, Andrew Bard Schmookler argues that the tobacco industry deceived the public by downplaying the health risks of smoking. Tobacco companies, in his opinion, are therefore partly responsible for influencing people's decision to smoke and should be held liable for the health costs of smoking. Schmookler is the author of *Living Posthumously: Confronting the Loss of Vital Powers*.

As you read, consider the following questions:

1. In what way is the tobacco industry similar to Shakespeare's Iago, in Schmookler's opinion?
2. What is the author's proposal for assessing the awards in lawsuits against tobacco companies?
3. According to Schmookler, why did tobacco companies reject the idea of honestly reporting on the health effects of smoking?

Reprinted from "Calculating the Individual's Cost of Smoking," editorial by Andrew Bard Schmookler, *Christian Science Monitor*, April 22, 1997, by permission of the author.

As the settlement negotiations between the US's two largest tobacco companies and the federal government suggest, the tobacco industry's position is becoming increasingly indefensible.

Yet some commentators are still asserting that the industry should be able to maintain its immunity to liability claims by individuals. The states may be able to sue successfully for their tobacco-related Medicare costs, this argument goes. But individuals should remain unsuccessful in the courts because it has long been known that smoking is bad for one's health, and people are responsible for their own choices. This reasoning lets the tobacco companies too easily off the moral and legal hook.

I'll concede that individual smokers must bear responsibility for their own choices. (Let's disregard for this discussion the Liggett Group's admission that the industry targeted minors, people whom we regard as less than fully responsible for their choices, in order to lure them into nicotine addiction.) But the logical fallacy is to leap from the idea that the smoker is responsible to the conclusion that therefore the industry is free of responsibility.

A Shakespearean Lesson

Responsibility is not an all-or-nothing thing. The hit man is certainly responsible for the murder he commits, but so is the guy who hired him. Rioters can be prosecuted for their mayhem, but "incitement to riot" is also—rightly—considered a crime.

And when it comes to the use of deception and manipulation to seduce others into making wrong choices, we in the audience of William Shakespeare's *Othello* think Othello, while also blaming himself for his unjust killing of the fair Desdemona, is justified when he runs his sword through the deceitful Iago.

As is evident in the Liggett documents, tobacco companies are in the position of Iago. For decades, they worked to create false confidence in the minds of smokers.

It is only partly true that everyone "knew" what they needed to know about tobacco to make responsible choices. As with responsibility, so also is "knowing" a matter of degree. True, there were scientific studies and then warning labels on cigarette packs. But there were also doubts—deliberately and deceptively planted. And these doubts had effects on what people "knew" and thus on the decisions they made. If there were no such effects, then what was the point of the industry spending so many millions to spread their false assurances?

That whole campaign of deliberate disinformation noted in the Liggett settlement—about tobacco's addictive nature and its health effects—would have been a foolish waste of money. And whatever else the tobacco defenders may be, they are not fools when it comes to the spending and making of their money.

The tobacco industry's deception, shown so clearly in the Liggett agreement, had effects, and these effects hurt the people deceived. We as a society cannot afford to say that those who perpetrated such destructive deception have no moral or legal responsibility to those injured.

THE TOBACCO INDUSTRY DESERVES BLAME

There is merit to the philosophy that we largely determine our own fate. In the case of cigarettes, this philosophical attitude would ring true only if there were a serious effort to restrict children's access to smoking; if the full spectrum of smoking's health risks were well known and widely publicized; and if cigarette companies were held to the same risk-disclosure standards as the rest of American manufacturers.

Elizabeth M. Whelan, *Priorities*, vol. 7, no. 2, 1995.

OK, you may say, so they are responsible. But if the smokers and the tobacco companies are both responsible, how do we handle the awards in suits in a situation as ambiguous as this? Do we just split the damages 50–50, or 25–75, or vice versa? Wouldn't any appointment be arbitrary?

Good questions—and I have a proposed answer.

What is needed is that we make an assessment: By what proportion would the sale of cigarettes in America have been reduced if the tobacco industry had owned up to the deceit Liggett now reveals about the health-related effects of its products? Not an entirely easy question to answer, perhaps, but an approximate judgment can be made.

After all, as industry documents now reveal, the tobacco companies contemplated taking the honest course and rejected it because of their calculations of how much business it would cost. Perhaps we can find these figures and use them.

THE PRICE OF DECEPTION

If we find such an estimate, we can solve the problem of apportionment. The portion of cigarette consumption that results from industry deception could be used as an index. It would show how much of the damage done by cigarettes can be laid at the door of the deceivers—rather than at the door of those who were influenced by the lies when they chose to smoke.

That percentage, then, could become a key to assessing damages (other than punitive) for which tobacco companies should be held liable to an individual smoker. If total damages to an individual can be documented, and deception is estimated to have boosted sales by 10 percent, the companies' responsibility would be one-tenth in that case.

In a morally sound society, people must pay the consequences of their own bad decisions. But that includes not only those who foolishly make self-destructive choices. It also includes those who selfishly—for their own profit—manipulate other people to do such foolish and self-destructive things.

> "Smokers are at least partially—if
> not mostly—responsible for the
> puffs they have taken."

PEOPLE ARE RESPONSIBLE FOR CHOOSING TO SMOKE

Richard B. McKenzie

In the following viewpoint, Richard B. McKenzie argues that smokers, not tobacco companies, should shoulder most of the responsibility for damaged health brought about by smoking. According to McKenzie, smokers freely make the decision to smoke. Therefore, he maintains, the tobacco industry should not be held liable for the future health care costs of smokers. McKenzie is a professor in the graduate school of management at the University of California in Irvine.

As you read, consider the following questions:

1. In McKenzie's opinion, what are some indicators that people make their own choices to smoke?
2. Why should teenagers be held responsible for their own decisions to smoke, in the author's opinion?
3. How could denying consumer culpability in smoking actually discourage people from quitting cigarettes, according to McKenzie?

Reprinted from "Tobacco Deal: Legal Mugging by Government," by Richard B. McKenzie, Los Angeles Times, Column Right, July 15, 1997, by permission of the author.

The tobacco companies now will pay dearly for their past economic sins. The claim of the state attorneys general and plaintiffs' lawyers who brought suits is straightforward: The tobacco industry caused hundreds of billions of dollars in health care expenditures. It should be held responsible for the financial drain that smoking has caused. Smokers are unwitting "victims" of tobacco company exploits.

Few seem willing to question the rhetorical foundation of the suits and claims, which seems to be no more sophisticated than, "The devil (meaning tobacco companies) made me do it."

SMOKERS HAVE A CHOICE

I do not smoke and never have, and I have no tie to the tobacco industry. I have no problem with the charge that smoking impairs health. But that doesn't mean that I and other reasonable Americans must drop our policy scruples and blindly accept the plaintiffs' claims. Clearly, the tobacco companies have contributed to the poor health of smokers. The companies made the "weeds" and encouraged people to smoke. People, however, had to buy them, so surely the smokers are at least partially—if not mostly—responsible for the puffs they have taken.

Granted, smoking is addictive to some degree, but that doesn't mean that individuals can shift all responsibility for their health problems to the tobacco companies. The fact that millions of people have kicked the habit indicates that a degree of choice plays a role in people's decisions to smoke. Moreover, addicted smokers were not always so: At some point, they had a choice about whether to go down the addictive path of smoking.

True, many people start smoking when they are teenagers, when, perhaps, their judgment may be impaired. But that doesn't mean that teenagers should not share responsibility for the damage they do to themselves. We hold teenagers responsible for their reckless driving for a simple reason: Absolving them of responsibility can increase their reckless driving. Similarly, pretending that the tobacco companies are totally responsible for teenage smoking can increase teenage smoking.

ENCOURAGING SMOKING

Without the admission of some choice in the matter, anti-smoking campaigns are a complete waste of time and money. Moreover, any complete denial of consumer choice may, inadvertently, cause fewer people to endure the stress of trying to quit smoking. They could reason, "Because my efforts will be in vain, there is no reason to even try." Anti-smoking campaigns, then, suggest that liability for smoking choices must be shared by consumers.

By allowing "society" to pick up part or all of the health care costs of smoking, the federal and state governments have lowered the cost of smoking and have encouraged smoking. States have, in effect, been in cahoots with tobacco firms to increase smoking and attendant state-subsidized health care costs.

Smokers Are Aware of Health Dangers

Tobacco industry critics assert that smoking is both addictive and harmful and must be additionally restricted by law. But like "addicted" runners and pastry eaters, smokers themselves can decide to restrict their own consumption when they estimate that the costs of their activity begin to outweigh the benefits.

It is simply not credible to maintain that smokers have been unaware of the long-term health risks of their habit or that they cannot change their behavior. The fact that Americans have quit smoking in droves over the last 20 years is demonstrable evidence to the contrary.

Dominick Armentano, *New American*, October 13, 1997.

The attorneys general obviously are pleased that they will make those who have gained from cigarette sales pay for the past health care expenditures. However, the payments ultimately will be claimed not from "companies," but from their current stockholders, many of whom bought their shares at prices inflated by the fact that they did not anticipate the health care claims. Many of the stockholders who gained from smoking long ago sold their stock for a profit. Similarly, current smokers will be forced to pay through higher prices for the health care costs of past smokers. Does that sound like ad hoc justice or what?

An Easy Target

The attorneys general are attacking the tobacco companies for a simple reason: They are an easy target. The attorneys don't have the political guts to go after the smokers with equal ferocity. But principle requires that we not single out groups for the imposition of health care damages just because they happen to be, for now, from the wrong side of the political tracks. Chocolate and potato chip companies sell products that may be as addictive to some consumers as tobacco is for others, and chocolate and chips very likely have hastened the deaths of tens of thousands of Americans. So should Hershey and Frito-Lay be subjected to suits for the considerable health care damage they (and their customers) have inflicted on the country because of the excess weight people carry?

Critics may say, "But tobacco is more harmful than chocolate and chips." Maybe so. But in trying to retain the resemblance of a free society, should we not seek to lean over backward and then some in allowing firms and consumers to do what they please, for good and bad reasons? If we don't, does not the tobacco deal look suspiciously like a legal mugging?

"Let them [the tobacco industry] face their day in court."

LAWSUITS AGAINST TOBACCO COMPANIES ARE JUSTIFIED

Elizabeth M. Whelan

In June 1997, the tobacco industry and several state attorneys general reached a tentative settlement—subject to approval by Congress—in response to lawsuits filed on behalf of individuals and groups who claim their health has been harmed by smoking. Part of this settlement would require tobacco companies to pay compensatory damages to states for health costs; in return, the tobacco industry would be granted immunity from future lawsuits. In the following viewpoint, Elizabeth M. Whelan argues that such a settlement would be counterproductive. According to Whelan, removing the threat of future litigation would release tobacco companies from their responsibility for the dangerous consequences of smoking. In her opinion, lawsuits against the tobacco industry are justified because tobacco companies have knowingly damaged public health. Whelan is president of the American Council on Science and Health, an association of scientists and doctors concerned with public health.

As you read, consider the following questions:

1. According to Whelan, how long have tobacco executives known about nicotine's addictiveness?
2. In what ways has Congress acted to the benefit of cigarette manufacturers, in the author's opinion?
3. What possible loopholes would allow the tobacco industry to avoid payment of monetary damages, according to Whelan?

From "Striking a Deal with Tobacco," by Elizabeth M. Whelan, *San Diego Union-Tribune*, June 29, 1997. Reprinted with permission of the American Council on Science and Health, 1995 Broadway, 2nd Floor, New York, NY 10023-5860.

It has been billed as a landmark deal, a breakthrough for public health, a way for state attorneys general who are suing the tobacco industry to recoup the medical costs of treating indigent smokers. But a look behind the facade of anti-tobacco hype reveals the truth about the tentative settlement reached in June 1997: This is a pro-cigarette pact, and it should be rejected.

REASONS TO REJECT THE SETTLEMENT

Here are ten reasons why:

1. It's the threatened tobacco industry, not the public health community, that has been pushing for a deal. Public health advocates have been winning major battles on both the local and national levels. Potentially effective class action, private, and criminal lawsuits have been launched across the nation. A court has ruled that the Food and Drug Administration (FDA) can regulate nicotine as a drug. At the local level vending machines are being prohibited and cigarette advertising near schools is being banned. And newly released internal industry documents have confirmed what we have always suspected: that even as they have publicly denied it, cigarette-company executives have known since the 1950s that nicotine is addictive and that cigarettes are dangerous.

2. The proposed deal was negotiated in a highly secret manner by people (the attorneys general) who are not motivated primarily by public health interests. Indeed, their dramatic pursuit of Big Tobacco casts attorneys general (AGs) with political aspirations in high-profile "good-guy" roles. Bringing home some big bucks after a showdown settlement will advance their ambitions. Clearly, it is acceptable for the AGs, either individually or collectively, to settle their own state lawsuits with the cigarette industry. But these state AGs have no legal or moral authority to make national public health policy by tying their settlement to concessions that will affect all Americans—whether inside or outside their states—for generations to come.

PROFITING FROM CIGARETTES

3. While the AGs have presented this deal as one severely punitive to big tobacco ("a very bitter pill for the industry," some deal proponents have termed it), the agreement will ultimately serve, not to impede, but to guarantee the future viability of the cigarette industry. A case in point: When the prospect of a deal was first rumored, cigarette stock prices soared.

4. The deal has basically nothing to do with public health. Martin Broughton, the chairman of England's BAT/Brown &

Williamson, summarized the situation perfectly when he quipped, "they want to be paid off and we want a peaceful life." The settlement involves the industry's distributing a lot of money to a lot of different players and then returning to business as usual, with the new players greedily sharing in the profits derived from cigarettes. (And remember: These are compensatory, not punitive, damages, which means that they are fully tax deductible. Half the industry's costs gets passed along to taxpayers.)

LEGAL PROTECTION FOR BIG TOBACCO?

5. In order to take effect, the proposed settlement must be approved by Congress, a body frequently described as the industry's "best filter yet." Because the U.S. Congress is friendly to tobacco, industry executives are eager to let the details of the settlement be resolved on that sympathetic turf. Congress has consistently passed legislation that benefits cigarette manufacturers at the expense of public health, starting with the passage of the 1965 act mandating government warning labels on cigarette packs—thereby absolving the industry of any obligation to warn consumers of the wide range of smoking's dangers, and—until the recent barrage of threatening lawsuits—affording the industry near-universal legal protection.

6. The deal is riddled with loopholes that provide the industry with ample opportunity for circumvention. For example, one clause dictates that the industry must pay strict monetary damages if there isn't a substantial drop in youth smoking. But the whole section is phrased in such a way as to excuse the companies from payment of damages if they can show that they tried their darndest and (dang it all!) those fool kids still insisted on smoking more than ever. Cartoon characters and familiar logos will be banned from cigarette ads; but the advertising geniuses will—as they have in Europe, where tobacco ads are already restricted—come up with innovative and effective new advertising campaigns, sans camels and sans cowboys.

7. For all practical purposes, the industry will never again have to worry about legal assaults: The deal will give it immunity from most lawsuits. For the industry, this immunity is the centerpiece of the deal. With the threat of litigation removed, the cigarette companies will have no incentive to behave responsibly. Why should they, when they will not be held accountable for the effects of their actions? There is a stark irony here: The industry will pay its compensatory damages and go back to business as usual. This is analogous to a scenario in which a cor-

poration admits to polluting the drinking water, pays some compensatory damages, and then—all guilt officially discharged—happily resumes dumping toxins down the well the very next morning, with no fear of the consequences.

ENDANGERING PUBLIC HEALTH

8. In return for the industry's being granted this invaluable immunity, the deal will garner the public health community some cash and a few concessions—concessions that already have been given or that are likely to evolve over time even without this deal. Other than the cash payoffs (which may rightfully earn this settlement the dubious title of "Drugs-for-Cash Deal of the Century"), there is little sympathy shown in the deal for those on the anti-smoking side. Instead, the cigarette lords will distribute lots of money to silence and pacify critics, who then become behind-the-scenes shareholders in the profits of big tobacco.

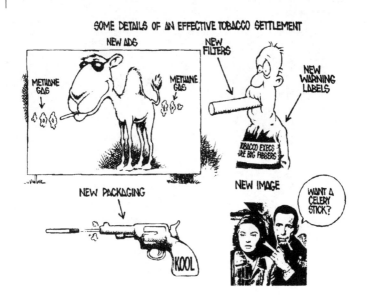

Tom Meyer, for the *San Francisco Chronicle*. Reprinted with permission.

9. All efforts to discourage smoking and to curb the outrageous behavior of an industry that is literally selling death will come to a screeching halt if this so-called settlement is put in place. The take-home message will be, "Well, now the cigarette problem is taken care of—let's get on with other issues." Nearly

500,000 Americans each year will continue to die prematurely from cigarettes, and there is no reason to believe that we will see any decrease in the numbers of children taking up smoking. By effectively ending the dialogue on the number-one public health problem in America, this settlement will leave future public health efforts in a state of paralysis.

SAY NO TO THE DEAL

10. Finally, if Congress passes this settlement, it will preserve —even enhance—the "supralegal," or above-the-law, status that Congress has already granted to the tobacco industry. For decades the cigarette has enjoyed a unique position—one that is the envy of all other industries. Cigarette companies don't have to test their ingredients, don't have to provide full-label disclosure, don't even have to tell the truth before Congress.

Let's for once treat the cigarette companies as we do every other industry. Scrap the deal and let them face their day in court.

| "We seem determined to reduce ourselves to a nation of children, prevented from making adult decisions about our own health and welfare."

LAWSUITS AGAINST TOBACCO COMPANIES ARE NOT JUSTIFIED

Stephen Chapman

Lawsuits against cigarette manufacturers for the monetary recovery of health damages are not justified, argues Stephen Chapman in the following viewpoint. He points out that smokers freely choose to smoke; furthermore, he contends, the tobacco industry cannot be accused of misrepresenting the hazards of smoking because the public has long been aware of these dangers. Instead of holding the tobacco industry liable for the hazards of smoking, Chapman maintains, people must accept responsibility for their own decisions to consume health-damaging products. Chapman is a nationally syndicated columnist.

As you read, consider the following questions:

1. Each year, how many Americans quit smoking, according to Chapman?
2. In the author's opinion, what could states have done to curb smoking?
3. According to Chapman, how do smokers save society money?

From "The Enemies of Tobacco Pose Their Own Risks," by Stephen Chapman, syndicated column, *Conservative Chronicle*, May 7, 1997. Reprinted by permission of Stephen Chapman and Creators Syndicate.

In the popular mind, tobacco companies are the embodiment of evil: big, wealthy, secretive, deceitful and dangerous. So when the major cigarette makers began peace talks with the people suing them, offering to pay out hundreds of billions of dollars in compensation and accept strict regulation of their industry, few voices were heard in their defense. The only concern was expressed by anti-tobacco groups worried that the merchants of death may be getting off too easy.

But Americans shouldn't be sanguine about the prospect of Big Tobacco being pounded into submission by an alliance of anti-smoking activists, federal regulators and plaintiffs' lawyers. The war on tobacco industry is also a war on the right of individuals to make their own choices—and their obligation to take responsibility for the consequences. And the movement, you can be sure, won't stop with tobacco.

Harmful Products Are Not Unusual

Cigarettes are dangerous products, causing a great deal of disease and death every year. In that, though, they are not unusual. Plenty of companies make money selling goods and services that carry serious risks—including 130-proof whiskey, trips up Mount Everest and cars that can travel three times the legal speed limit. But we don't let the family of a Corvette owner sue Chevrolet because he got killed trying to take a turn too fast.

Why is the tobacco business treated as somehow unique? One excuse is that its executives have misrepresented the dangers of smoking. That might constitute fraud—if anyone with detectable brain activity believed the lies and acted on that belief. But the connection between tobacco and premature death has been a matter of common knowledge for generations. A 1949 Gallup poll found that even then, most smokers regarded cigarettes as harmful. Suing the tobacco industry for misrepresented the dangers of their product is akin to joining the Flat Earth Society and then asking for damages when you discover that the planet is actually round.

People Choose to Smoke

The assumption in most discussions is that smokers are helpless slaves to their addiction. True, smoking does create physical dependence, but 1.2 million Americans manage to quit every year—and two-thirds of the people who have ever smoked no longer do. Tossing the word "addiction" around doesn't change the basic fact that people smoke of their own free will. Smokers smoke because they value the satisfactions of smoking more than they fear its hazards.

The current negotiations stem mainly from a horde of lawsuits by state governments trying to recover the alleged costs of caring for indigent citizens injured by tobacco. That's another red herring. If smokers cost states excessive amounts of Medicaid funds, why not sue the smokers or refuse to pay their medical bills? They, too, are to blame for the costs of smoking.

The states involved in the lawsuits are also guilty. If they thought smoking was too costly a vice to indulge, they could have banned it—instead of milking it for billions in tax revenue. They could also have acted vigorously to prevent sales to minors, something most have done only in recent years.

Hitch. Reprinted with special permission of North America Syndicate.

But the surprising truth is that, on balance, the government doesn't lose money from the ravages of smoking. Everyone on Medicaid or Medicare, sad to say, eventually dies of some ailment that the state will have to cover. For non-smokers, the costs are postponed a bit, but not reduced or averted.

Smokers, however, yield savings elsewhere. Every smoker who makes his exit at age 60 instead of 80 reduces spending on Social Security and other pension payments. Duke University economist W. Kip Viscusi says that in monetary terms, society gains more than it loses from smoking—even without counting the taxes paid on cigarette sales.

THE PRICE OF AVOIDING RESPONSIBILITY

If tobacco companies should be held liable for the medical consequences of decisions made by competent adults, why not other corporations? Obesity is an even bigger public health problem. McDonald's and Burger King sell fat-drenched fare that many people find impossible to resist even though it may someday kill or cripple them. These companies also brazenly target children. It's not far-fetched to think that in 10 years, plaintiffs' lawyers and state attorneys general will be in court demanding reparations from the fast-food industry.

Here's the right way to settle the issue: Let cigarette companies sell their products to willing adults, and pass a law barring them from having to pay damages to individuals or states for the normal, foreseeable health consequences of smoking.

That, of course, is not likely to happen. We seem determined to reduce ourselves to a nation of children, prevented from making adult decisions about our own health and welfare and expecting someone else to bear responsibility anytime we make foolish mistakes. We can fleece Big Tobacco, but the rest of us will also pay a high price.

> "[The proposed tobacco settlement]
> must aim not only to reduce youth
> smoking, but to meet other health
> goals as well."

THE PROPOSED TOBACCO
SETTLEMENT WOULD BENEFIT
PUBLIC HEALTH

Bill Clinton

In the following viewpoint, Bill Clinton voices his support for
the proposed tobacco settlement that would include tobacco-
industry payments to states to compensate for the costs of treating smoking-related disease, funding for antismoking programs,
regulation by the Food and Drug Administration, and restrictions on advertising. Clinton argues that such legislation is especially necessary to protect youths from the dangers of tobacco
and to safeguard the health of future generations. This viewpoint
is excerpted from a September 17, 1997, news conference in
which Clinton discussed the tobacco settlement originally proposed in June 1997. Clinton is the forty-second president of the
United States.

As you read, consider the following questions:

1. According to Clinton, what is the stated goal of the Food and
   Drug Administration's effort to reduce youth smoking?
2. What is one of the best ways to help reduce teen smoking,
   according to the author?
3. In Clinton's opinion, why must the tobacco settlement
   protect tobacco farmers?

Reprinted from "Remarks by the President on Tobacco Settlement Review," by Bill Clinton,
Office of the Press Secretary, at www.whitehouse.gov/WH/New/html/tobaccorem.html,
September 17, 1997.

This is a time of prosperity and hope and optimism for America, with our economy improving, making progress on our social problems, our efforts to lead the world to a more prosperous and peaceful future making headway. But I think we all know that this country still has some significant challenges, especially in the health field. And if we think about what we want America to be like in the 21st century, the health of our people and especially the health of our children must be paramount in our thinking, in our vision, and in our efforts.

That's why, [in 1996], I worked with the Food and Drug Administration (FDA) and we launched this nationwide effort to protect our children from the dangers of tobacco by reducing youth access to tobacco products and by preventing companies from advertising to our children.

The purpose of the FDA rule was to reduce youth smoking by 50 percent within seven years. Earlier [in 1997], a federal judge in North Carolina said that the FDA has the authority to regulate tobacco products to protect the health of our children. There have also been other examples of litigation progress, as you know, brought by private plaintiffs and by the Attorneys General. Now, these victories for public health drove the tobacco companies to the bargaining table. They extracted concessions that would have been literally unthinkable just a short time ago.

An Unprecedented Opportunity

I want to say a special word of thanks to the Attorneys General and the other parties who worked hard to negotiate this settlement. Everyone knows we would not be here had it not been for their foresight, their determination, and their relentless efforts.

Now we have this unprecedented opportunity to enact comprehensive tobacco legislation, working with all the parties involved—the members of Congress, the attorneys general, the representatives of injured parties, the public health community, the tobacco farmers and others. We have moved from confrontation and denial and inertia to the brink of action on behalf of our children, and that is all to the good.

Today [September 17, 1997] I want to challenge Congress to build on this historic opportunity by passing sweeping tobacco legislation that has one goal in mind: the dramatic reduction of teen smoking. In the coming weeks I will invite congressional leaders from both parties to the White House to launch a bipartisan effort to enact such legislation.

There are five key elements that must be at the heart of any national tobacco legislation. Reducing teen smoking has always been America's bottom line. It must be the industry's bottom line. That is why I believe the first thing any tobacco legislation must include is a comprehensive plan to reduce teen smoking, including tough penalties. These penalties should be non-tax-deductible, uncapped, and escalating to give the tobacco industry the strongest possible incentive to stop targeting children as new customers.

THE NEED TO REDUCE TEEN SMOKING

The focus on teenagers is due, in part, to the fact that about one-half of adult smokers become regular smokers by age 18. In a summary of the 1994 Surgeon General's report, Joycelyn Elders et al. noted that nearly all first use of tobacco occurs prior to high school graduation. These authors also reported that the rate of increase in teenage smoking has not declined in the past few years, despite substantial declines in smoking in the population at large. A 1994 Centers for Disease Control and Prevention report confirms that smoking among teenagers has actually increased during the past decade. One policy implication of these reports is that smoking morbidity and mortality can be reduced significantly if teenagers' access to cigarettes is limited.

Peter D. Jacobson and Jeffrey Wasserman, *Tobacco Control Laws: Implementation and Enforcement*, 1997.

One of the surest ways of reducing youth smoking is to increase the price of cigarettes. Today I call for a combination of industry payments and penalties to increase the price of cigarettes by up to a dollar and a half a pack over the next decade, as needed, to meet our youth reduction targets. And I call upon the House to follow the lead of the United States Senate and repeal the provision giving the tobacco industry a $50 billion tax credit.

HOLDING THE TOBACCO INDUSTRY ACCOUNTABLE

Second, any legislation must affirm the full authority of the FDA to regulate tobacco products. I believe the FDA's jurisdiction over tobacco products must be as strong and effective as its authority over drugs and devices. In particular, legislation cannot impose any special procedural hurdles on the FDA's regulation of tobacco products.

Third, effective legislation must include measures to hold the industry accountable, especially in any efforts to market products to children, while insisting on changes in the way it does business. I ask the industry again to make a voluntary commitment to stop advertising to children. And I call upon Congress to pass legislation providing for broad document disclosure so that the public can learn everything the tobacco companies know about the health effects of their products and their attempts to market to our children.

Fourth, federal tobacco legislation must aim not only to reduce youth smoking, but to meet other health goals as well. These include the reduction of secondhand smoke, the expansion of smoking prevention and cessation programs, the strengthening of international efforts to control tobacco, and the provision of funds for medical research and other important health objectives. We must build on the bipartisan agreement to fund children's health care in the recent balanced budget.

And finally, any tobacco legislation must protect tobacco farmers and their communities. We know that tobacco farmers are honest, hard-working people, most of whom live and work on small, family-owned farms. In some states, entire communities rely on income from the tobacco crop. Any legislation must protect these farmers, their families and their communities from loss of income. . . .

BUILDING THE FUTURE OF THE NATION

And finally, let me say again, we wouldn't be here if it weren't for all the people in this room and the countless others they represent around the country. To me, this is not about money. It is not about how much money we can extract from the tobacco industry. It is about fulfilling our duties as parents and responsible adults to protect our children and to build the future of this country. We are doing everything we can in this administration to give parents the tools they need to raise their children, but parents have to be our partners as well. If this is not just about money, we have to recognize that even beyond the tobacco companies and all of us in this room, every parent in America has a responsibility to talk to their children about the dangers of tobacco, illegal drugs, and other things that can hurt them. We know if we have strong parental responsibility here, they can make a great deal of difference in protecting our children as well.

If we take responsibility, if we pass this legislation, if we do what we should here, if the tobacco industry will work with us, if other members of Congress in both parties will work with us, we will have gone a very long way toward creating the state of health for our children that will make America an even greater nation in the new century.

"The unhappy prospect [of the proposed tobacco settlement] is yet more incursions by a nanny state with an insatiable appetite for social engineering."

THE PROPOSED TOBACCO SETTLEMENT THREATENS LIBERTY

Robert A. Levy

In the following viewpoint, Robert A. Levy argues against a proposed settlement that would require the tobacco industry to pay compensatory health damages, restrict marketing, submit to regulation by the Food and Drug Administration, and fund antismoking campaigns. In Levy's opinion, such a settlement would give the government too much power over private industry and would limit individual choice—setting a dangerous precedent that could lead to more state controls over individual liberty. He concludes that the courts—not the government—should handle disputes between private parties and the tobacco industry. Levy is a senior fellow in constitutional studies at the Cato Institute, a libertarian research foundation in Washington, D.C.

As you read, consider the following questions:

1. In Levy's opinion, what is wrong with the proposal to have tobacco companies reimburse states for the Medicaid costs of smoking-related diseases?
2. What harmful side effects could result from restricting cigarette sales, according to Levy?
3. In the author's opinion, what evidence proves that cigarette advertising does not encourage youths to smoke?

Reprinted, with permission, from "A Tobacco Settlement That Is Dangerous to Our Liberty," editorial by Robert A. Levy, *San Diego Union-Tribune*, July 22, 1997.

The he tobacco settlement is a shameful proposal, extorted by public officials who have perverted the rule of law to tap the deep pockets of an unpopular industry. In a 68-page "Proposed Resolution," the industry agreed to pony up $370 billion, submit to Food and Drug Administration (FDA) regulation, and rein in certain sales and marketing practices. In return, tobacco companies will be exempt from punitive damages for past conduct and immune from new class-action lawsuits.

CONSUMERS' CLAIMS MUST BE PROVEN

Part of the monetary settlement is to fund kids' health insurance, anti-smoking campaigns, even programs to help kick the habit. But why should tobacco companies be responsible for these crusades? After all, cigarettes are legal; the choice to smoke is freely made. Claims that some consumers are hopelessly addicted, having relied on fraudulent information and deceptive advertising, must be proven in a court of law.

Those claims cannot be resolved by legislative fiat or by negotiation at gunpoint. And to hold a single industry financially liable because some families are unable or unwilling to insure their offspring is quite simply intolerable.

Moreover, there is no justification whatsoever for the largest component of the monetary settlement, reimbursement of state Medicaid outlays. To fatten their own coffers, states have sued to recover expenditures for Medicaid recipients with "tobacco-related diseases"—without even showing that an injured party smoked, or that smoking caused his illness. Furthermore, authoritative studies have concluded that excise taxes on cigarettes already exceed public costs attributable to smoking.

A NANNY STATE

If the tobacco industry were the only victim of this settlement, that would be bad enough; but the unhappy prospect is yet more incursions by a nanny state with an insatiable appetite for social engineering.

Under the Proposed Resolution, the FDA can ban nicotine after the year 2009, more conspicuous warnings will appear on each pack of cigarettes, and smoking will be prohibited in most public and work places. Right around the corner are similar restrictions on alcohol, diet drinks, dairy products, fast food—you name it. And once the state gets its nose into our business, we should not be surprised at pernicious side effects, including a flourishing black market and rampant crime.

The proposed settlement also contains Draconian restrictions on advertising and merchandising. Vending machine sales are prohibited. Text-only, black-and-white ads are the rule. Billboards are proscribed. Joe Camel and the Marlboro Man are history; no more merchandise with tobacco logos; no more sponsorship of athletic events.

THE TOBACCO DEAL AND THE SLIPPERY SLOPE

Clearly the country has committed itself to an ideology of victimology without bounds. With the [proposed] tobacco deal we slide much farther down the slippery slope into complete surrender to Big Nanny and the nitwit Left. Manifestly, the powers that be in this country have abandoned all belief in individual responsibility. In view of their strong desire for enslavement, Americans do not deserve our sympathy. They deserve exactly what they are clamoring for, and they are well on the way to getting it good and hard.

Robert Higgs, Liberty, September 1997.

It doesn't take a constitutional scholar to conclude that these rules are ridiculous. We protect gangsta rap from the censors, for example, despite its message to youngsters that the drug culture is admirable and killing police officers is a pleasurable recreational activity. Yet if Tiger Woods shows up wearing a Joe Camel tie tack, our speech guardians will see to it that R.J. Reynolds is prosecuted. Will the Budweiser frogs be next to croak? Shall we muzzle Red Dog beer ads?

HEALTH IS NOT THE REAL CONCERN

Even if we believe that tobacco companies have targeted underage prospects, they clearly have not accomplished their objective. Over the 1985–95 decade, during the heyday of Joe Camel, the percentage of kids aged 12–17 who smoke dropped from 29 percent to 20 percent, with even steeper reductions among minorities.

Longer-term, the average age of first-time cigarette users has neither advanced nor declined from 1962 through the latest 1994 data. Some ads may have succeeded in gaining brand share, but they have been singularly unsuccessful in expanding the overall market.

Make no mistake, dollars and cents—not health issues—are the driving force behind the settlement. Both federal and state governments opt for financial health over smokers' health when their money is on the line.

Facing claims by military personnel for tobacco-related illnesses, Veterans Affairs secretary Jesse Brown told former soldiers to pay their own freight for having chosen to smoke.

When sued by a prisoner who was denied a nicotine patch for the habit he developed in a Florida jail, the state insisted it was no more responsible for his purchase of cigarettes than for his "buying a candy bar at the canteen." If that principle renders the government immune from liability, it renders private companies immune as well.

APPLY THE RULE OF LAW

The correct disposition of the "Proposed Resolution" is one that ex-presidential candidate Steve Forbes suggested for the tax code: Kill it, drive a stake through its heart, bury it and start over.

Disputes between private parties cannot be resolved in secret negotiations involving defendants who have the boot of government pressing on their necks, state attorneys general who seek to replenish their Medicaid coffers without fiscal discipline, contingency fee lawyers who wield the sword of the state while retaining a financial interest in the outcome, and advocacy groups that have subordinated the rule of law to their health concerns, however well-intentioned.

Our courts, not our legislatures, are constituted to deal with these matters; but they can do justice only if the rule of law—objective and evenhanded—is scrupulously applied.

PERIODICAL BIBLIOGRAPHY

The following articles have been selected to supplement the diverse views presented in this chapter. Addresses are provided for periodicals not indexed in the *Readers' Guide to Periodical Literature*, the *Alternative Press Index*, the *Social Sciences Index*, or the *Index to Legal Periodicals and Books*.

Jonathan Alter	"Smoking Out What's Cool," *Newsweek*, June 30, 1997.
Jeffrey H. Birnbaum	"Tobacco's Can of Worms," *Fortune*, July 21, 1997.
John Carey et al.	"Not So Fast," *Business Week*, July 7, 1997.
Susan Crabtree	"Failure to Play Straight Clouds Tobacco's Future," *Insight*, June 16, 1997. Available from 3600 New York Ave. NE, Washington, DC 20002.
Stanton A. Glantz et al.	"Looking Through a Keyhole at the Tobacco Industry: The Brown and Williamson Documents," *JAMA*, July 19, 1995. Available from Subscriber Services Center, American Medical Association, 515 N. State St., Chicago, IL 60610.
Matthew Miller	"Clean Lungs at a Price: Do Smoking-Related Deaths Save the Nation Money?" *U.S. News & World Report*, July 7, 1997.
Mother Jones	Special report on the politics of tobacco, May/June 1996.
Timothy Noah	"A Hit or a Miss for Mr. Butts?" *U.S. News & World Report*, June 30, 1997.
Peter Pringle	"Billboard Wars: The Battle over Tobacco Rages On as the Industry Suppresses Information and Muzzles Criticism," *Index on Censorship*, July/August 1996.
Jill Smolowe	"Sorry, Pardner," *Time*, June 30, 1997.
Elizabeth M. Whelan	"Is a Deal with the Cigarette Industry in the Interest of Public Health?" *Priorities*, vol. 9, no. 2, 1997. Available from the American Council on Science and Health, 1995 Broadway, 2nd Fl., New York, NY 10023-5860.

FOR FURTHER DISCUSSION

CHAPTER 1

1. The American Thoracic Society argues that cigarette smoking is harmful to human health; Rosalind B. Marimont and Charley Reese contend that the dangers attributed to smoking have been exaggerated. What evidence does each author present to support his or her argument? Which author's evidence do you find more convincing? Explain.

2. Clifford E. Douglas maintains that nicotine makes tobacco products highly addictive. Richard J. DeGrandpre asserts that factors other than nicotine could make cigarettes habit forming. How do the arguments of these two authors reflect differing views on the nature of addiction?

3. After reading the viewpoints by John R. Garrison and Jacob Sullum, are you more or less likely to support restrictions on cigarette smoking in public places? Explain your reasoning.

4. The Office of the Surgeon General contends that the use of chewing tobacco and snuff can lead to cancer, heart disease, and nicotine addiction. Brad Rodu and Philip Cole argue that smokeless tobacco products could alleviate the symptoms of nicotine withdrawal while smokers try to quit. On what points do the authors agree? On what points do they disagree?

CHAPTER 2

1. According to William Everett Bailey and Ronald M. Davis, cigarette advertising is specifically designed to encourage children to start smoking. To prevent or reduce teen smoking, they contend, tobacco advertising must be restricted. How do Ernest Beck, James K. Glassman, and Jacob Sullum respond to this argument?

2. Barbara Dority contends that limiting or banning cigarette ads is a violation of free speech. The organization Action on Smoking and Health maintains that advertising is restricted for many legal goods and services. Which viewpoint do you find most convincing? Why?

CHAPTER 3

1. Randolph D. Smoak Jr. and M. Lester O'Shea differ over the seriousness of environmental tobacco smoke and how people should respond to its dangers. In your opinion, which argument is most convincing? Explain your answer.

2. Michael Grossman and Frank J. Chaloupka argue that increasing the taxes on cigarettes would be the most effective way to reduce teen smoking. Stephen Gold contends, however, that a cigarette tax is an unfair burden on poor smokers and could lead to a black market. Do you think Gold's fears are warranted? Why or why not? Based on your reading of the viewpoints in this book, what measures would reduce teen smoking? Support your answer with examples from the viewpoints.

CHAPTER 4

1. Elizabeth M. Whelan argues that lawsuits against the tobacco industry are justified because cigarette companies have knowingly damaged public health. Stephen Chapman disagrees, arguing that the tobacco industry is not liable for health damages because people have long been aware of the dangers of smoking. Based on the authors' arguments, do you believe that cigarette manufacturers should be held liable for smoking-related illnesses? Why or why not?

2. The viewpoints in this chapter include several perspectives on the proposed settlement that would require tobacco companies to pay compensatory health damages to states and grant the tobacco industry immunity from future lawsuits. Consider each perspective and then list arguments for and against each one. Note whether the arguments are based on facts, values, emotions, or other considerations. If you strongly agree or disagree with a perspective, explain why.

ORGANIZATIONS TO CONTACT

The editors have compiled the following list of organizations concerned with the issues debated in this book. The descriptions are derived from materials provided by the organizations. All have publications or information available for interested readers. The list was compiled on the date of publication of the present volume; the information provided here may change. Be aware that many organizations take several weeks or longer to respond to inquiries, so allow as much time as possible.

Action on Smoking and Health (ASH)
2013 H St. NW, Washington, DC 20006
(202) 659-4310 • fax: (202) 833-3921
web address: http://www.ash.org
Action on Smoking and Health promotes the rights of nonsmokers and works to protect them from the harms of smoking. It provides scientific, educational, legal, and advocacy services; strives to ban tobacco ads from radio and television; and encourages the establishment of no-smoking sections on airplanes, trains, and buses. ASH publishes the bimonthly newsletter *ASH Smoking and Health Review* and fact sheets on a variety of topics, including nicotine addiction, passive smoking, and the costs of workplace smoking.

American Cancer Society
PO Box 142302, Austin, TX 78714-2302
(800) 227-2345
web address: http://www.cancer.org
The American Cancer Society is one of the primary organizations in the United States devoted to educating the public about cancer and to funding cancer research. The society spends a great deal of its resources on educating the public about the dangers of smoking and on lobbying for antismoking legislation. The American Cancer Society publishes hundreds of publications, ranging from reports and surveys to position papers.

American Council on Science and Health (ACSH)
1995 Broadway, 2nd Fl., New York, NY 10023-5860
(212) 362-7044 • fax: (212) 362-4919
web address: http://www.acsh.org
ACSH is a consumer education group concerned with issues related to food, nutrition, chemicals, pharmaceuticals, lifestyle, the environment, and health. It publishes the quarterly *Priorities* as well as the booklets *The Tobacco Industry's Use of Nicotine as a Drug* and *Marketing Cigarettes to Kids.*

American Lung Association (ALA)
1740 Broadway, New York, NY 10019-4374
(212) 315-8700 • fax: (212) 265-5642
e-mail: info@lungusa.org • web address: http://www.lungusa.org

Founded in 1904, the American Lung Association is the oldest voluntary health agency in the United States. It is dedicated to the prevention, cure, and control of all types of lung disease, including asthma, emphysema, tuberculosis, and lung cancer. ALA's mission is to prevent lung disease and to promote lung health.

Americans for Nonsmokers' Rights
2530 San Pablo Ave., Suite J, Berkeley, CA 94702
(510) 841-3032 • fax: (510) 841-7702
e-mail: anr@no-smoke.org • web address: http://www.no-smoke.org

Americans for Nonsmokers' Rights seeks to protect the rights of nonsmokers in the workplace and other public settings. It works with the American Nonsmokers' Rights Foundation, which promotes smoking prevention, nonsmokers' rights, and public education about involuntary smoking. The organization publishes the quarterly newsletter *ANR Update*, the book *Clearing the Air*, and the guidebook *How to Butt In: Teens Take Action*.

California Smokers' Helpline
English hot line: (800) 7-No Butts (766-2888)
Spanish hot line: (800) 45-No Fume (456-6386)

The California Smokers' Helpline provides one-on-one telephone counseling in an effort to help both adolescents and adults kick the habit of cigarette smoking. Clients receive follow-up sessions as needed for relapse prevention. The hot line provides callers with appropriate literature and a list of local resources for further assistance in quitting smoking.

Canadian Council on Smoking and Health (CCSH)
170 Laurier Ave. West, Suite 1000, Ottawa, ON K1P 5V5, CANADA
(613) 567-3050 • fax: (613) 567-2730

CCSH is a national nonprofit organization that works to achieve a tobacco-free society in Canada. It coordinates national antitobacco activities and promotes a comprehensive tobacco control program involving educational, social, fiscal, and legislative interventions designed to reduce tobacco use in Canada. CCSH publishes the *Smoking or Health Update* three times a year as well as various fact sheets, pamphlets, and resource kits.

Competitive Enterprise Institute (CEI)
1001 Connecticut Ave. NW, Suite 1250, Washington, DC 20036
(202) 331-1010 • fax: (202) 331-0640
e-mail: info@cei.org • web address: http://www.cei.org

The institute is a pro–free market public interest group involved in a wide range of issues, including tobacco. CEI questions the validity and accuracy of Environmental Protection Agency studies that report the dangers of secondhand smoke. Its publications include the monthly newsletter *CEI Update* and numerous books, monographs, and policy studies.

Environmental Protection Agency (EPA)

Indoor Air Quality Information Clearinghouse
PO Box 37133, Washington, DC 20013-7133
(800) 438-4318 • (202) 484-1307 • fax: (202) 484-1510
e-mail: iaqinfo@aol.com • web address: http://www.epa.gov/iaq/

The EPA is the agency of the U.S. government that coordinates actions designed to protect the environment. It promotes indoor air quality standards that reduce the dangers of secondhand smoke. The EPA publishes and distributes reports such as *Respiratory Health Effects of Passive Smoking: Lung Cancer and Other Disorders* and *What You Can Do About Secondhand Smoke as Parents, Decisionmakers, and Building Occupants* as well as the fact sheet *Setting the Record Straight: Secondhand Smoke Is a Preventable Health Risk*.

Fight Ordinances & Restrictions to Control & Eliminate Smoking (FORCES)

PO Box 591257, San Francisco, CA 94159
(415) 824-4716
web address: http://www.forces.org

FORCES fights against smoking ordinances and restrictions that are designed to eventually eliminate smoking, and it works to increase public awareness of smoking-related legislation. It opposes any state or local ordinance that it feels is not fair to those who choose to smoke. Although FORCES does not advocate smoking, it asserts that an individual has the right to choose to smoke and that smokers should be accommodated where and when possible. FORCES publishes *Tobacco Weekly* as well as many articles.

Foundation for Economic Education

30 S. Broadway, Irvington-on-Hudson, NY 10533
(914) 591-7230 • fax: (914) 591-8910
e-mail: freeman@westnet.com • web address: http://www.fee.org

The foundation promotes private property rights, the free market economic system, and limited government. Its monthly journal, the *Freeman*, has published articles opposing regulation of the tobacco industry.

Group Against Smokers' Pollution (GASP)

PO Box 632, College Park, MD 20741-0632
(301) 459-4791

Made up of nonsmokers adversely affected by tobacco smoke, GASP works to promote the rights of nonsmokers, to educate the public about the problems of secondhand smoke, and to encourage the regulation of smoking in public places. The organization provides information and referral services and distributes educational materials, buttons, posters, and bumper stickers. GASP publishes booklets and pamphlets such as *The Nonsmokers' Bill of Rights* and *The Nonsmokers' Liberation Guide*.

Tobacco Merchants Association of the United States
PO Box 8019, Princeton, NJ 08543-8019
(609) 275-4900 • fax: (609) 275-8379
e-mail: tma@tma.org

The association represents manufacturers of tobacco products; tobacco leaf dealers, suppliers, and distributors; and others related to the tobacco industry. It tracks statistics on the sale and distribution of tobacco and informs its members of this information through the following periodicals: the weekly newsletters *Executive Summary, World Alert*, and *Tobacco Weekly*; the biweekly *Leaf Bulletin* and *Legislative Bulletin*; the monthly *Trademark Report* and *Tobacco Barometer: Smoking, Chewing & Snuff*; and the quarterly newsletter *Issues Monitor*. The association has a reference library, offers on-line services, and provides economic, statistical, media-tracking, legislative, and regulatory information.

U.S. Food and Drug Administration (FDA)
Rockville, MD 20857
(800) 532-4440 • (301) 443-1130 • fax: (301) 443-9767
e-mail: execsec@oc.fda.gov • web address: http://www.fda.gov

As the agency of the U.S. government charged with protecting the health of the public against impure and unsafe foods, drugs, cosmetics, and other potential hazards, the FDA has sought the regulation of nicotine as a drug and has investigated manipulation of nicotine levels in cigarettes by the tobacco industry. It provides copies of congressional testimony given in the debate over regulation of nicotine.

BIBLIOGRAPHY OF BOOKS

William Everett Bailey   *The Invisible Drug.* Cincinnati, OH: Mosaic, 1996.

John C. Burnham   *Bad Habits: Drinking, Smoking, Taking Drugs, Sexual Misbehavior, and Swearing in America.* New York: New York University Press, 1993.

California Environmental Protection Agency   *Health Effects of Exposure to Environmental Tobacco Smoke: Final Report.* Sacramento, CA: The Office, 1997.

Karen Casey   *If Only I Could Quit: Recovering from Nicotine Addiction.* Center City, MN: Hazelden, 1995.

Maurice Duke   *Tobacco Merchant: The Story of Universal Leaf Tobacco Company.* Lexington: University Press of Kentucky, 1995.

John Fahs   *Cigarette Confidential: The Unfiltered Truth About the Ultimate American Addiction.* New York: Berkeley, 1996.

Food and Drug Administration   *Regulation of Cigarettes and Smokeless Tobacco Under the Federal Food, Drug, and Cosmetic Act.* Washington, DC: Department of Health and Human Services, USFDA, 1996.

A. Lee Fritschler   *Smoking and Politics: Policy Making and the Federal Bureaucracy.* Upper Saddle River, NJ: Prentice Hall, 1996.

Timothy L. Gall and Daniel M. Lucas, eds.   *Statistics on Alcohol, Drug, and Tobacco Use: A Selection of Statistical Charts, Graphs, and Tables About Alcohol, Drug, and Tobacco Use from a Variety of Published Sources with Explanatory Comments.* Detroit, MI: Gale Research, 1996.

David G. Gilbert   *Smoking: Individual Differences, Psychopathology, and Emotion.* Washington, DC: Taylor and Francis, 1995.

Stanton A. Glantz   *The Cigarette Papers.* Berkeley and Los Angeles: University of California Press, 1996.

Mark S. Gold   *Tobacco.* New York: Plenum Medical, 1995.

Emma Haughton   *A Right to Smoke?* New York: Watts, 1997.

Philip J. Hilts   *Smokescreen: The Truth Behind the Tobacco Industry Cover-Up.* Reading, MA: Addison-Wesley, 1996.

Peter D. Jacobson   *Tobacco Control Laws: Implementation and Enforcement.* Santa Monica, CA: RAND, 1997.

Richard Klein   *Cigarettes Are Sublime.* Durham, NC: Duke University Press, 1993.

Richard Kluger   *Ashes to Ashes: America's Hundred-Year Cigarette War, the Public Health, and the Unabashed Triumph of Philip Morris.* New York: Knopf, 1996.

Susan S. Lang and Beth H. Marks	*Teens and Tobacco: A Fatal Attraction.* New York: Twenty First Century Books, 1996.
Barbara S. Lynch and Richard J. Bonnie, eds.	*Growing Up Tobacco Free: Preventing Nicotine Addiction in Children and Youths.* Washington, DC: National Academy Press, 1994.
Jim McCormick	*Light Up and Live: Intelligent Guide to Safer Smoking.* Chicago: Brighton Press, 1989.
Daniel McMillan	*Teen Smoking: Understanding the Risks.* Springfield, NJ: Enslow, 1997.
National Cancer Institute	*The FTC Cigarette Test Method for Determining Tar, Nicotine, and Carbon Monoxide Yields of U.S. Cigarettes: Report of the NCI Expert Committee.* Bethesda, MD: U.S. Department of Health and Human Services, 1996.
C. Tracy Orleans and John Slade, eds.	*Nicotine Addiction: Principles and Management.* New York: Oxford University Press, 1993.
Richard Peto et al.	*Mortality from Smoking in Developed Countries, 1950–2000: Indirect Estimates from National Vital Statistics.* New York: Oxford University Press, 1994.
Robyn Richmond, ed.	*Interventions for Smokers: An International Perspective.* Baltimore, MD: Williams & Wilkins, 1994.
Elizabeth M. Whelan, ed.	*Cigarettes: What the Warning Label Doesn't Tell You: The First Comprehensive Guide to the Health Consequences of Smoking.* Amherst, NY: Prometheus Books, 1997.
World Health Organization	*Tobacco or Health: A Global Status Report.* Geneva: World Health Organization, 1997.

INDEX